GOD'S WILL FOR OUR LIVES

GOD'S WILL FOR OUR LIVES

by

JACK HARTMAN

New Leaf Press
P.O. BOX 311, GREEN FOREST, AR 72638

FIRST EDITION
1989

Library of Congress Catalog Number: 89-060441
ISBN: 0-89221-167-9

Cover Design - Bonnie Curnock

Typesetting - A.G.A.P.E. Graphics

Contents

Introduction

The Master Designer of the universe has a definite plan for each person He has created. As we start to mature spiritually, many of us ask questions such as "Why am I here?", "What does God want me to do with my life?" and "How can I find meaning, purpose and fulfillment in my life?".

All of us want God's best for our lives. There is a simple way to receive this - to find His plan for our lives, enter into it and remain in it. I have spent many hours studying God's Word to find everything I could concerning this vital subject.

This book is solidly anchored in the Holy Scriptures. I have done my best to write upon a difficult subject in a clear and easy-to-understand style. I pray that this book will open tremendous new horizons for you and that it will help you to find God's will for your life.

1

God Has A Plan For Every Person

Before we were formed in our mothers' wombs, God already had a specific plan for each of our lives: "Before I formed you in the womb I knew and approved of you [as My chosen instrument], and before you were born I separated and set you apart, consecrating you..." (Jeremiah 1:5, *The Amplified Bible*)

This is a great spiritual truth. Before any of us were conceived, God knew us intimately and gave His approval to our lives. Before we were born, He had a special plan for each of our lives - a plan that set us apart from everyone else.

Long before we were born, He had a very clear vision of what He wanted us to accomplish with our lives: "You saw me before I was born and scheduled each day of my life before I began to breathe. Every day was recorded in Your Book!" (Psalms 139:16, *The Living Bible*)

Our Father knows each of us much better than we can ever know ourselves. He knows exactly what we are like deep down in our hearts. He knows everything we do. He knows every thought that passes through our minds. He even knows what we are going to say before we say it!

"O Lord, You have examined my heart and know everything about me. You know when I sit or stand. When far away You know my every thought. You chart the path ahead of me, and tell me where to stop and rest. Every moment, You know where I am. You know what I am going to say before I even say it." (Psalms 139:1-4, *The Living Bible*)

Isn't it wonderful to realize that the same Almighty God who created every planet, star and galaxy in the universe knows each of us so intimately? Our Father is very interested in each of us. We are very special to Him. He took infinite care in creating us.

He decided who our parents would be, whether we would be male or female and where we would be born. He chose the color of our skin, eyes and hair. He determined who our brothers and sisters would be or whether we would be an only child. His plan for our lives includes our personality, our abilities and our intelligence.

Each of us is unique. No two people are alike, even identical twins. We're not here by chance. Our Creator gave each of us unique talents to carry out the mission He has for us: "...Christ has given each of us special abilities - whatever He wants us to have out of His rich storehouse of gifts." (Ephesians 4:7, *The Living Bible*)

There is no doubt that God has a specific plan for each of us. However, Satan also enters into the picture. Before our salvation, we were children of Satan and our lives were greatly influenced by him: "You are of your father the devil; and it is your will to practice the lusts and gratify the desires [which are characteristic] of your father..." (John 8:44, *The Amplified Bible*)

Even though God has a plan for each of us before we are born, we cannot fulfill His will until we are set free from sin: "...they will come to their senses and escape from Satan's trap of slavery to sin which he uses to catch them whenever he likes, and then they can begin doing the will of God." (II Timothy 2:26, *The Living Bible*)

In spite of this, there are many times before we are saved when God intervenes in our lives. Even though we are technically children of Satan before we are saved, God is still omnipotent and has great influence over our lives. If He didn't, Satan would destroy us.

Every person who has ever been reborn spiritually was drawn towards salvation by God Himself. Jesus said, "No one is able to come to Me unless the Father Who sent Me attracts and draws him and gives him the desire to come to Me..." (John 6:44, *The Amplified Bible*)

When we are set free from sin, our Father wants us to surrender every area of our lives to His will: "...give yourselves completely to God - every part of you - for you are back from death and you want to be tools in the hands of God, to be used for His good purposes." (Romans 6:13, *The Living Bible*)

This is the reason we are here on earth after we are saved. If God didn't have a specific plan for the remainder of our lives, He would take us immediately to heaven after our salvation. While we are waiting to leave this earth and live eternally in heaven, we should continuously seek God's will for our lives.

He didn't leave us here to seek pleasure and live our lives the way we want to live them. Jesus Christ paid a tremendous price for us so that we could be used as channels for Him. He wants to be more than our Saviour. He also wants to be Lord of our lives. He cannot be Lord unless we follow His instructions: "...why call ye me, Lord, Lord, and do not the things which I say?" (Luke 6:46, *The King James Bible*)

If Jesus truly is our Lord, we will deny ourselves and put Him first each day of our lives. We will continuously strive to draw closer to Him so we can carry out His will: "...'Anyone who wants to follow Me must put aside his own desires and conveniences and carry his cross with him every day and keep close to Me!' " (Luke 9:23, *The Living Bible*)

Jesus knows the way. He'll show us if we let Him. We say "yes" to Him the day we are reborn spiritually. He wants us to keep on saying "yes" throughout every day of our lives.

He wants to be Lord of our lives the first thing in the morning, all day long and the last thing before we go to sleep at night.

He has given us the wisdom we need to find His will: "...He lavished upon us in every kind of wisdom and understanding (practical insight and prudence), making known to us the mystery (secret) of His will - of His plan, of His purpose..." (Ephesians 1:8-9, *The Amplified Bible*) He has provided everything we need to carry out His will: "...may the God of peace, who brought again from the dead our Lord Jesus, equip you with all you need for doing His will..." (Hebrews 13:20, *The Living Bible*)

The same God Who created us will guide us in every area pertaining to His will for our lives. Would He create us and then leave us alone in this cruel world with no help to carry out His will? Of course not! He has provided everything we will ever need.

Our generation lives in the last days before the return of Jesus Christ. It is especially important for us to seek the Lord's will and carry it out: "Look carefully then how you walk! Live purposefully and worthily and accurately, not as the unwise and witless, but as wise - sensible, intelligent people; making the very most of the time - buying up each opportunity - because the days are evil. Therefore do not be vague and thoughtless and foolish, but understanding and firmly grasping what the will of the Lord is." (Ephesians 5:15-17, *The Amplified Bible*)

The Lord wants our lives to be worthwhile. He doesn't want us wasting our lives as many people do. Our remaining time on earth is precious. It is very important for each of us to make a conscious decision to spend our days doing what He wants us to do until Jesus returns: "Teach us to number our days and recognize how few they are; help us to spend them as we should." (Psalms 90:12, *The Living Bible*)

There is much to be done. Our Lord has chosen to use human vessels to do His work. His eyes continuously scan the globe looking for Christians who sincerely want to be His channel: "...the eyes of the Lord search back and forth across the whole earth, looking for people whose hearts are perfect towards Him, so that He can show His great power in helping them..." (II Chronicles 16:9, *The Living Bible*)

It's interesting to see that He continually looks across the entire world. Some of us may not be fully dedicated to seeking His will the first few times He looks. Then, through a book such as this or through another catalyst, when His eyes scan the globe again, I believe He will find more people who are devoted above all else to finding His will for their lives.

It's not too late! We shouldn't feel guilty if we haven't found God's will at this point in our lives. Helping us find His will is like everything else He does. We go through stages until He works us into a position where we are able to hear His voice and carry out His will.

I encourage each reader of this book. The following pages contain specific instructions to help you spend the remainder of your days on earth finding God's will for your life, entering into it and remaining in it.

2

Jesus Christ And His Father's Will

I believe all Christians would agree Jesus Christ is our model. He is our example in every area. The best way to see how important it is to seek God's will is to examine how important this was to Jesus during His earthly ministry.

Adam and Eve resisted God's will. As a result, they lost the precious relationship they had with God. Jesus Christ, the second Adam, didn't fall into this trap. He resisted His own will at all times. He always submitted to His Father's will.

The following illustration shows this clearly: "...the disciples urged Him saying, Rabbi, eat something. But he assured them, I have food (nourishment) to eat of which you know nothing and have no idea. So the disciples said one to another, Has someone brought Him something to eat? Jesus said to them, My food (nourishment) is to do the will (pleasure) of Him Who sent Me and to accomplish and completely finish His work." (John 4:31-34, *The Amplified Bible*)

This shows that many of us look for satisfaction in the natural realm when we should seek it in the spiritual realm.

We are fed spiritually to the degree we are committed to carrying out God's will. This will "fill us up" spiritually in a manner that cannot be accomplished through food or any other worldly desire.

Jesus knew this. He realized the futility of trying to accomplish personal goals. This is why He said, "...the Son is able to do nothing from Himself - of His own accord..." (John 5:19, *The Amplified Bible*) If the greatest person who ever walked the face of this earth could do nothing of Himself, why would any of us think we should try to accomplish our goals with our limited human abilities?

Shortly after this, Jesus again emphasized that He could do nothing by Himself and expounded even more on this. He said, "I am able to do nothing from Myself - independently, of My own accord - but as I am taught by God and as I get His orders. [I decide as I am bidden to decide. As the voice comes to Me, so I give a decision.] Even as I hear, I judge and My judgment is right (just, righteous), because I do not seek or consult My own will - I have no desire to do what is pleasing to Myself, My own aim, My own purpose - but only the will and pleasure of the Father Who sent Me." (John 5:30, *The Amplified Bible*)

We can learn a great deal from this statement. If Jesus did nothing independently of God, we should do the same. He said He made no decisions without seeking His Father's guidance. He had no desire to do what pleased Him. He knew He could depend on His Father to show Him His will. We will only find true meaning and fulfillment in our lives to the degree we sincerely seek to carry out God's will.

Jesus had only one goal when He came from heaven to earth. This was to turn away from His own desires and to focus entirely on carrying out His Father's will: "For I have come down from heaven, not to do My own will and purpose, but to do the will and purpose of Him Who sent Me." (John 6:38, *The Amplified Bible*)

We see a further example of our Lord's commitment to carry out His Father's will in the crisis He went through in the garden of Gethsemane. Jesus knew His betrayal by Judas was close at hand. He knew the horrible physical suffering that awaited Him. Even worse, He knew that He, the pure and sinless Christ, would have to become sin.

It is important to realize that Jesus was the Son of man at this time. He was a human being just like we are. He had the same potential to become fearful that we do. He knew He needed strength from His Father. With full realization of what faced Him, "...He threw Himself upon the ground on His face and prayed saying, My Father, if it is possible, let this cup pass away from Me; nevertheless, not what I will - not what I desire - but as You will and desire." (Matthew 26:39, *The Amplified Bible*)

How would any of us react if we were 33 years old and faced a horrible, gruesome death by crucifixion? How would we react if we were pure and sinless and still had to become black with the sins of all mankind? Wouldn't we agonize over this horrible fate? Wouldn't we try to see if there was any other way out?

Of course we would. Jesus was human just as we are. He went through tremendous agony as He struggled with the decision of carrying out His Father's will. He dreaded what was ahead of Him. He thought of turning back. He wanted to get out of this ordeal if He could.

Jesus agonized so much over this decision that He actually sweat blood: "...He was in such agony of spirit that He broke into a sweat of blood, with great drops falling to the ground as He prayed more and more earnestly." (Luke 22:44, *The Living Bible*)

The agony of this decision was so great that Jesus suffered from a medical condition known as "haemitidrosis." People suffer from this when stress is so great that it causes their blood vessels to break and blood is excreted through the sweat glands.

This is the price Jesus had to pay to carry out His Father's will. Even at this traumatic time He was able to turn away from His will to carry out His Father's will.

A tremendous spiritual battle was fought that night in the garden of Gethsemane. This battle was fought for us. Our eternal life hung in the balance. Fortunately for us Jesus decided to do His Father's will.

After Gethsemane He went through three separate trials before Jewish and Roman officials. He was judged guilty even though there was not one shred of evidence against Him. He then was "scourged" by Roman soldiers. He was stretched out naked and whipped across the back with a whip consisting of several leather thongs with jagged pieces of bone and metal tied to the end.

Scourging is too horrible to describe. When it was completed, Jesus was "...beaten and bloodied, so disfigured one would scarcely know it was a person standing there..." (Isaiah 52:14, *The Living Bible*)

Think of this. Jesus Christ - God Himself - was stripped naked. He was whipped so brutally that the flowing blood and horrible wounds disfigured Him so much He didn't even look like a human being any more!

This was just the beginning of the price He paid for us. After this horrible ordeal and a sleepless night, He was forced to carry a heavy wooden cross through the streets of Jerusalem to the place of His execution. After this long and weary journey Jesus and His captors finally arrived at the place where He was to be executed. He was stretched out naked and forced to lie flat on His back on a large wooden cross lying on the ground. Four Roman soldiers held Him down while another soldier nailed Him to the cross with five-inch spikes.

Can you imagine the pain of having a five-inch spike driven through the palm of each hand? It usually took four to five blows with a hammer to nail each hand to the cross. This process was then repeated as spikes were driven into each foot. The pain of being nailed to a cross was so great that many criminals fainted.

The cross was then lifted into place. For three hours Jesus hung there surrounded by jeering, obscene crowds of people. He went through agonizing thirst. He ached in every bone and muscle more than we could begin to understand. The agony of death by crucifixion is beyond our comprehension.

However, Jesus paid a price that was even greater than the price of scourging and crucifixion. The perfect sinless One Who had never sinned actually became sin for each of us: "...God took the sinless Christ and poured into Him our sins..." (II Corinthians 5:21, *The Living Bible*)

To us scourging would have been unbearable. To us crucifixion is beyond comprehension. However, to the perfect sinless Christ, to become sin was the worst penalty of all. He paid the price for our sins. He paid a debt He did not owe. We owe a debt we cannot pay.

The Bible doesn't explain how this process of becoming sin took place. Bible scholars surmise that the scene of the sinless Christ partaking of the sins of all mankind was so horrible that His Father was unable to look and turned away from His Son.

Can we even begin to comprehend how Jesus must have felt after going through immense agony in the natural realm and even worse suffering in the spiritual realm only to realize that His Father had turned His back upon Him? This is why He cried out, "...My God, My God, why have You abandoned Me - leaving Me helpless, forsaking and failing Me in My need? (Matthew 27:46, *The Amplified Bible*)

This is the price Jesus had to pay to carry out His Father's will. Just before dying on the cross, "...He said, It is finished! and He bowed His head and gave up His spirit." (John 19:30, *The Amplified Bible*) Jesus said, "It is finished" because, at that moment, everything He had been sent to earth to accomplish had been successfully carried out.

This is why we are told in The Lord's Prayer that we should always do God's will: "...Thy will be done in earth, as it is in heaven." (Matthew 6:10, *The King James Bible*) God's will is always done in heaven. We should strive to do His will here on earth just as Jesus did His Father's will during His earthly ministry.

If we truly want to be members of the family of Jesus Christ, we must do our very best to carry out God's will: "For whosoever shall do the will of my Father which is in heaven, the same is my brother, and sister, and mother." (Matthew 12:50, *The King James Bible*)

We were sent to earth for the same reason Jesus was - not to do our own will, but the will of the One Who sent us: "I have given you an example to follow: do as I have done to you." (John 13:15, *The Living Bible*)

If we can only begin to catch a glimpse of the magnificent sacrifice Our Lord made for us, our adoring hearts should overflow continuously with gratitude. How can we presume to believe we have the right to live our lives the way we want to live them?

Jesus paid an enormous price for our lives: "You were bought with a price - purchased with a preciousness and paid for [by Christ]..." (I Corinthians 7:23, *The Amplified Bible*) Our lives are not our own. They belong to Jesus Christ.

We must not get caught up with our plans, goals and desires. We don't have the right to live the way we want to live: "We are not our own bosses to live or die as we ourselves might choose. Living or dying we follow the Lord. Either way we are His." (Romans 14:7-8, *The Living Bible*)

Our Father loves us so much that He willingly gave up His only Son for all of us while we were still sinners. Jesus loves us so much that He sweat blood, was beaten, whipped and crucified and became sin for us. We should love Him so much that we are willing to devote our lives to carry out His will.

We sin when we do our own will instead of His will. He died for us. We should live for Him. Too many of us are on the throne of our own lives. We need to get off the throne and put Jesus there.

We must not try to take His place. If we try to control our lives, we are trying to do what He has earned the right to do. He didn't believe His life was too much to give up for us. The least we can do is to give up our lives for Him.

3

Love, Humility And God's Will

We grieve our Father's heart if we insist on seeking our own goals. If we do this, we deny the very purpose we were created for. Unfortunately, because many of us insist on running our own lives, we have to go through the painful process of being broken from our own desires.

Before a horse can be ridden, it has to be broken. We are no different. If we insist upon our own will, many of us will have to be humbled and broken in order to come to the point where we voluntarily seek God's will for our lives.

He has a definite plan for each of us, but we can only find this plan if we are humble: "...walk (lead a life) worthy of the [divine] calling to which you have been called - with behavior that is a credit to the summons to God's service, living as becomes you - with complete lowliness of mind (humility) and meekness (unselfishness, gentleness, mildness), with patience, bearing with one another and making allowances because you love one another." (Ephesians 4:1-2, *The Amplified Bible*)

These verses of Scripture tell us that our Father wants us to lead our lives in a manner worthy of His divine calling. How do we do this? We do this by being humble, unselfish, gentle and patient. We do this by reaching out to others in love.

Many of us miss God's will for our lives because we fail to love others. When we treat other human beings in this way, we are doing exactly what Satan wants. He knows this attitude brings us into his darkness and keeps us out of the light our Father wants us to be in:

"Anyone who claims to be in the light but hates his brother is still in the darkness. Whoever loves his brother lives in the light, and there is nothing in him to make him stumble. But whoever hates his brother is in the darkness and walks around in the darkness; he does not know where he is going, because the darkness has blinded him." (I John 2:9-11, *The New International Version*)

Love is the cornerstone of Christianity. Without it, we are spiritually dead: "We know that we have passed over out of the death into the Life by the fact that we love the brethren, [our fellow Christians]. He who does not love abides - remains, is held and kept continually - in [spiritual] death." (I John 3:14, *The Amplified Bible*)

God and love are one and the same. If we don't love others, we cannot know God because God is love. If we cannot know God, we cannot know His will: "...those who are loving and kind show that they are the children of God, and that they are getting to know Him better. But if a person isn't loving and kind, it shows that he doesn't know God - for God is love." (I John 4:7-8, *The Living Bible*)

Many of us don't know how to love others and what it means to love someone else. Some people view love as an emotion. However, Christian love is an action. It is unconditional. God loves us unconditionally. There are "no strings attached" to His love for us. He wants us to love others unconditionally. Jesus explained this when He said,

"There is a saying, 'Love your friends and hate your enemies.' But I say: Love your enemies! Pray for those who persecute you! In that way you will be acting as true sons of your Father in heaven. For He gives His sunlight to both the evil and the good, and sends rain on the just and on the unjust too. If you love only those who love you, what good is that? Even scoundrels do that much. If you are friendly only to your friends, how are you different from anyone else? Even the heathen do that. But you are to be perfect, even as your Father in heaven is perfect." (Matthew 5:43-48, *The Living Bible*)

Our human love is not sufficient to love other people who are very difficult to love. God gave us His supernatural love so that we could love all people unconditionally: "...God's love has been poured out in our hearts through the Holy Spirit Who has been given to us." (Romans 5:5, *The Amplified Bible*)

When we love others with unconditional love, this enables us to draw closer to God and to better understand His ways. This, in turn, enables us to be in a better position to find His will for our lives.

Unconditional love and humility are only possible to the degree the Holy Spirit is in control of our lives. Nothing can begin to compare to a life that is directed by the Holy Spirit. It is beautiful beyond description because the Holy Spirit doesn't do things the way we do. His ways are vastly different from ours.

Our Father will never try to force us to do His will. The only way we can find His will is to come to Him with humble hearts. This opens the door for His guidance: "He leads the humble in what is right, and the humble He teaches His way." (Psalms 25:9, *The Amplified Bible*)

None of us would knowingly put ourselves in a position that would cause Almighty God to be in direct opposition to us. However, this is exactly what we do when we are proud: "...God sets Himself against the proud and haughty, but gives grace [continually] to the lowly - those who are humble-minded [enough to receive it]." (James 4:6, *The Amplified Bible*)

When we are humble and realize how lowly we truly are,

this opens the door for us to continually receive blessings that we have not earned and do not deserve. If we truly want to find meaning in our lives, we must realize how insignificant we really are in our own selves. "Humble yourselves - feeling very insignificant - in the presence of the Lord, and He will exalt you. - He will lift you up and make your lives significant." (James 4:10, *The Amplified Bible*)

Our Father rewards His humble and obedient children. He blesses us when we turn away from the pridefulness of our will and submit ourselves before Him by continually seeking His will. Pride is never within the will of God. Prideful actions put us right in the center of Satan's will. Satan appeals to our pride. He wants us to glorify ourselves.

Satan continually tries to weave a subtle web of deception to cause us to do what we want to do. He was successful in doing this with Adam and Eve. He failed to deceive Jesus Christ.

He has been trying to get human beings to seek their own will for many years. He knows very well what happens to us when we are proud: "Pride goeth before destruction, and an haughty spirit before a fall." (Proverbs 16:18, *The King James Bible*)

At one time, Satan was an archangel. His name was Lucifer and he was very close to God. However, pride caused him to exalt his desires over God's. This caused Lucifer to fall from heaven and to be changed into Satan.

Because of this, Satan strives to get us to succumb to our prideful goals and desires. He wants pride to cause us to miss God's will for our lives just as it caused him to miss God's will.

One way that he does this is to place great emphasis on self-confidence and self-reliance. Many Christians fall into this trap even though the Word of God says "...we should not trust in ourselves..." (II Corinthians 1:9, *The King James Bible*)

Self-confidence and self-reliance are worldly traits. God's Word teaches us to have Christ-confidence and Christ-reliance. If we trust in ourselves instead of trusting in the

Lord, this makes it very difficult to find His will for our lives.

We must not be preoccupied with ourselves and our plans. We are warned against self-centeredness: "...I warn every one among you not to estimate and think of himself more highly than he ought - not to have an exaggerated opinion of his own importance..." (Romans 12:3, *The Amplified Bible*)

Our Father wants us to follow the guidance of the Holy Spirit. He doesn't want us to obstinately insist upon our own way. If we do this, we are like stubborn mules who are so headstrong they can only be controlled by a bit in their mouths.

"I will instruct you (says the Lord) and guide you along the best pathway for your life; I will advise you and watch your progress. Don't be like a senseless horse or mule that has to have a bit in its mouth to keep it in line!" (Psalms 32:8-9, *The Living Bible*)

I can tell you from personal experience how true this is. There have been many occasions in the ministry the Lord has given me when I received a clear vision from the Lord as to what He wanted me to do. Unfortunately, I have missed the mark on many occasions because I was so headstrong that I ran ahead of Him.

Instead of waiting on Him, I insisted on plunging ahead. In essence, I was saying, "Come on, Lord. Catch up to me." I have learned the hard way to wait on the Lord and never to rush ahead.

It's very easy to get ahead of God. Many "religious" people fall into this trap. They try very hard to do what they think God wants them to do. However, many of these people are using the energy of the flesh instead of the energy of the Holy Spirit.

If we do this we play right into the hands of Satan. One of his most effective traps is to tempt us to do what seems right to us instead of seeking God's will: "There is a way which seemeth right unto a man, but the end thereof are the ways of death." (Proverbs 14:12, *The King James Bible*)

Self-effort always leads to spiritual death. When we

plunge ahead doing what seems right to us, we diffuse the power of the Holy Spirit. It isn't released in our lives when we do what we think we should do. His power is released only when we humble ourselves before Him, wait on Him and seek His will.

4

We Must Crucify Our Personal Goals

God's ways are very different from our ways. In His kingdom, leaders are servants: "...whosoever will be great among you, let him be your minister; and whosoever will be chief among you, let him be your servant: even as the Son of man came not to be ministered unto, but to minister..." (Matthew 20:26-28, *The King James Bible*)

This doesn't come naturally to us. Our natural inclination is to do what we want to do: "...all seek [to advance] their own interests, not those of Jesus Christ, the Messiah." (Philippians 2:21, *The Amplified Bible*)

It's interesting to note that this verse of Scripture doesn't say some of us seek our own goals. It says "all" of us do this. We all inherit this predisposition to "do our own thing" from our ancestor Adam.

It's natural for us to want our own way. It's not natural to submit to others with a servant's attitude. This is especially true when we are young and headstrong.

However, as we grow older, we should become more

mature. As we mature, we should learn to turn away from our personal goals and desires and, instead, seek God's will in every area of our lives: "Shun youthful lusts and flee from them, and aim at and pursue righteousness - all that is virtuous and good, right living, conformity to the will of God in thought, word and deed..." (II Timothy 2:22, *The Amplified Bible*)

Instead of seeking our personal goals, we should "...be aglow and burning with the Spirit, serving the Lord." (Romans 12:11, *The Amplified Bible*) This is how the Lord wants us to live. He wants us to be on fire because our goals are submitted to the Holy Spirit as we serve the Lord under His guidance.

Our carnal nature craves recognition from others. The truth is that any glory Christians receive belongs to the Lord. We are not here to steal His glory. We are here to serve Him and to serve one another as channels of the Holy Spirit.

In God's kingdom, those who attain the highest rank are those who lower themselves the most. The more we chase after our personal goals and desires, the more we block the blessings our Father has for us. The more we deny these goals and desires and humble ourselves before God and one another, the more we open the door for blessings from our Father.

Jesus died so that we would turn away from our goals and submit our lives to Him: "...He died for all, so that all those who live might live no longer to and for themselves, but to and for Him Who died and was raised again for their sake." (II Corinthians 5:15, *The Amplified Bible*)

He fulfills His goals on earth through us. If our lives truly belong to Him, we will turn away from our goals: "...those who belong to Christ Jesus, the Messiah, have crucified the flesh - the Godless human nature - with its passions and appetites and desires." (Galatians 5:24, *The Amplified Bible*)

We sin if we seek personal goals. Sin is doing things our way instead of God's way. Sin tries to do God's work for Him. In the kingdom of God, power comes from crucifixion. The greatest power in the history of the universe came from the crucifixion of Jesus Christ. The power of the Holy Spirit is released in us and through us when we crucify our desires and yield to His desires.

Our will is spiritual death. God's will is spiritual life! We cannot come alive in the kingdom of God unless our desires are dead. Jesus said, "...If any one intends to come after Me, let him deny himself - forget, ignore, disown, lose sight of himself and his own interests - and take up his cross, and (joining Me as a disciple and siding with My party) follow with Me - continually, [that is,] cleave steadfastly to Me." (Mark 8:34, *The Amplified Bible*)

If we want to live our lives the way God wants us to, we must turn away from personal goals: "...learn to put aside your own desires so that you will become patient and godly, gladly letting God have His way with you." (II Peter 1:6, *The Living Bible*)

In the kingdom of God the pearl of great price is attained by giving up everything just as Jesus gave up everything. God, in His wisdom, made the abundant life available in the last place the logical intellectual mind would expect to find it.

It is available through Jesus Christ only to the degree we are able to crucify our desires. Our Lord wants us to be the clay. He wants us to allow Him to be the potter. He wants us to allow Him to mold us and use us in any way He wants.

There is nothing more beautiful to Jesus than a surrendered life. He wants us to share His crucifixion every day of our lives: "I have been crucified with Christ - [in Him] I have shared His crucifixion; it is no longer I who live, but Christ, the Messiah, lives in me; and the life I now live in the body I live by faith - by adherence to and reliance on and [complete] trust - in the Son of God, Who loved me and gave Himself up for me." (Galatians 2:20, *The Amplified Bible*)

This isn't easy to do. I try to do this every day of my life and I often fail. I go to the Lord many times each day, ask for His forgiveness and ask for a fresh start.

I'm not trying to tell you readers of this book that this will be easy for you either. However, God's Word does instruct us to share in the crucifixion of Christ. He lives inside of us. He wants to live His life in us and through us. He will do this to the degree we are truly able to let go and trust Him to control our lives.

Jesus isn't looking for our ability. Several of His disciples were modest, humble, unskilled fishermen. If we truly surrender our lives to the indwelling Christ, His ability becomes our ability, His energy becomes our energy and His will becomes our desire!

The key to entering into His will is for His will to become increasingly important while our personal goals become less important: "He must increase, but I must decrease - He must grow more prominent, I must grow less so." (John 3:30, *The Amplified Bible*)

Freedom in the kingdom of God is the opposite of freedom in the world. In the world, people think they are free when they are "doing their own thing." They are blind if they believe this. We are never less free than we are when we seek our own desires. Freedom in the kingdom of God comes from giving up our God-given right to do what we want to do and do what God wants us to do. Freedom comes from surrender!

All sin has its root in selfishness. Can you name any sin that doesn't have selfishness as its foundation? Because this is true we then can conclude that freedom from sin comes from selflessness. Self-centeredness leads us into bondage to Satan. God-centeredness sets us free.

If we truly seek God's will for our lives, we must die to our own desires. This is the most difficult battle I fight every day of my life. It is a continual battle. It is never completely won. Just when we believe we have victory, we find that we don't. Nevertheless, any Christian who truly seeks God's will must strive continually to die to personal goals and desires.

5

The Beauty Of God's Will

Some Christians are secretly afraid of God's will. It seems unattractive. We think God's will is going to be unpleasant and hesitate to seek it for this reason.

This is exactly what Satan wants us to think. He is the biggest liar of all time: "...there is no truth in him. When he speaks a falsehood, he speaks what is natural to him; for he is a liar [himself] and the father of lies and of all that is false." (John 8:44, *The Amplified Bible*)

Satan continually tries to put lies into our minds. This is his primary mission. He has been stripped of all spiritual power. His only hope is in his ability to deceive. He tries to deceive us into thinking God's will for our lives is unattractive. He wants us to be afraid of giving up our will and entering into God's will.

When someone speaks of giving up his own free will and surrendering his life to God's will, this sounds unattractive to the carnal mind. Satan knows this. He shudders in fear that we might come to understand the beauty of God's will and the ugliness of our will.

Who can control our lives better - God or us? He created us. Doesn't He know what is best for us? He loves us. We shouldn't be afraid of His will. Whatever He wants is best for us!

He will never force us to do anything. As we willingly surrender our lives to Him, He will cause His will to be our desire. We can trust our Father. He has our best interest at heart. Nothing can approach the magnificence of the fulfillment we will experience when we find His will for our lives, enter into it and remain in it.

His will isn't a burden. It will give meaning to our lives that cannot be found elsewhere. The most exciting place to be is in the very center of God's will for our lives! If we are able to remain in God's will, our lives will be more beautiful, meaningful and fulfilling than we could possibly imagine.

Let me give you an example from my own life. I have known for many years that God has called me to be an author of Christian books. Satan has tried in every possible way to destroy me and my ministry. I can't begin to tell you of many of the hardships I have endured because they are so personal.

Nevertheless, in the midst of all this pain and anguish, I have experienced deep inner contentment because I have known every step of the way that I was in the center of God's will. This sustained me when everything else was falling apart. The knowledge that I was in God's will shored me up and gave me the inner strength to keep on going. It opened the door to continuous guidance from the Holy Spirit when I desperately needed direction.

God's will is just as beautiful when we are in the valley as it is when we are on the mountaintop. Jesus explained how beautiful He wants our lives to be: "...I came that they may have and enjoy life, and have it in abundance - to the full, till it overflows." (John 10:10, *The Amplified Bible*)

Does this sound like something to fear or turn away from? Jesus came to earth so we could enjoy life. He came so we could find abundance. He came so our lives could be full and overflowing. His will is much more beautiful than our will could ever be!

Many of us are blind. We can't understand the heavy load we carry as we go through life carrying the burden of our goals and desires. When we get rid of this and seek the Lord's will for our lives, life is much better.

Everything any of us have ever wanted and much more can be ours if we seek God's will with all our hearts. If we could just get the slightest vision of how beautiful His will is, each of us would spend morning, noon and night seeking it.

All Christians should look forward to heaven. It's going to be more magnificent than we can possibly comprehend. Everyone will be happy and fulfilled there because everyone in heaven lives according to God's will. If we want to be happy and fulfilled here on earth, we must have this same goal.

If God's will is magnificent in heaven, it must be wonderful here on earth as well. I'm not in any way implying that life on earth at its best is anywhere near as wonderful as heaven is going to be. However, I believe we can experience a portion of the kingdom of heaven when we line up with God's will here on earth.

Although everyone does His will in heaven, He gives us a choice on earth. If we know we're going to do His will in heaven and if we know it is going to be wonderful there, why wouldn't we want to do His will during the remainder of our lives here on earth?

This world isn't our real home. We are just passing through. Heaven is our real home: "...you are only visitors here...your real home is in heaven..." (I Peter 2:11, *The Living Bible*)

When we get to heaven, we won't have any hesitation to do whatever our Father wants us to do. We should have this same attitude here on earth: "...whether we are at home [on earth away from Him], or away from home [and with Him], we are constantly ambitious and strive earnestly to be well-pleasing to Him." (II Corinthians 5:9, *The Amplified Bible*)

We can experience a small preview of the joy of heaven when we are able to forget what we want to do and continually seek the Lord's will here on earth. It is possible for us to enter into the kingdom of heaven while we are on earth! Our

Lord Jesus told us how to do this: "Not every one who says to Me, Lord, Lord, will enter the kingdom of heaven, but he who does the will of My Father Who is in heaven." (Matthew 7:21, *The Amplified Bible*)

Jesus said, "...the kingdom of God is within you." (Luke 17:21, *The King James Bible*) This is where the Holy Spirit lives: "Do you not know that your body is the temple - the very sanctuary - of the Holy Spirit Who lives within you?..." (I Corinthians 6:19, *The Amplified Bible*)

As long as we willingly and cheerfully surrender control of our lives to Him, He will reveal the beauty of God's will to us. If we turn to Him each day and seek God's will with all our heart, He will reveal it to us.

When God created us, He put in our hearts exactly what His will for our lives is. This is very much like a seed. It is planted within us just waiting to take root, grow and produce an abundant harvest of results.

He will produce this wonderful harvest when our lives are centered around Him and we desire His will more than anything else: "Delight yourself also in the Lord, and He will give you the desires and secret petitions of your heart." (Psalm 37:4, *The Amplified Bible*)

This is a conditional promise. It is possible for each of us to receive the desires we have deep down inside of ourselves. God promised to give these desires to us. However, we must meet His condition.

The condition is that we delight ourselves in Him. This means we should find joy and pleasure in finding what He wants us to do. This should transcend everything else. If we delight ourselves in Him and seek His will with all our hearts, He will give us our innermost desires.

If we truly do delight ourselves in Him, His desires will become our desires. He knows much better than we do what is best for us. Little children often want many things that aren't good for them, but their parents refuse to comply because they know what is really good for their children.

It's no different with our heavenly Father and His children. He will bless us beyond the limits of our comprehension if we humbly seek His will at all times. We must understand what He wants for us is much better than anything we would choose for ourselves.

If we have a deep desire to find His will and if this means more to us than anything else, He will reveal it to us: "...If you seek Him - inquiring for and of Him, and requiring Him as your first and vital necessity - you will find Him..." (I Chronicles 28:9, *The Amplified Bible*)

He knows exactly what He wants each of us to do: "For I know the plans I have for you, says the Lord. They are plans for good and not for evil, to give you a future and a hope. In those days when you pray, I will listen. You will find me when you seek me, if you look for me in earnest." (Jeremiah 29:11-13, *The Living Bible*)

We can see here that our Lord has promised His will is good for us. This should give us great optimism for our remaining years on earth. If we pray and ask Him to reveal His plans and if we seek them with all our hearts, He will listen to our prayers and reveal His plans to us.

I don't know about you, but this gives me great hope for the future. We live in uncertain times. From a worldly point of view there is much to be concerned about. However, from God's point of view, we can rest assured that His plans for the remainder of our lives are good, and we can look forward to carrying out these plans.

6

Do Not Conform To The World

In the next two chapters we'll focus primarily on the following verse of Scripture. It tells us a great deal about God's perfect will: "Do not be conformed to this world - this age, fashioned after and adapted to its external, superficial customs. But be transformed (changed) by the [entire] renewal of your mind - by its new ideals and its new attitude - so that you may prove [for yourselves] what is the good and acceptable and perfect will of God, even the thing which is good and acceptable and perfect [in His sight for you]." (Romans 12:2, *The Amplified Bible*)

In this chapter we'll discuss only the first portion of this verse of Scripture. It says we shouldn't conform to the external superficial customs of the world. The world's way of doing things is shallow and one dimensional because people who do not have a personal relationship with Jesus Christ have no spiritual understandiing.

Because of this, the ways of the world have no spiritual depth or meaning. They are based primarily upon external conditions. Our Father doesn't want us to fall into the trap of living the way unsaved people in the world live.

In fact, His Word even says that anyone who is caught up in the world's way of doing things is His enemy: "...Do you not know that being the world's friend is being God's enemy? So whoever chooses to be a friend of the world takes his stand as an enemy of God." (James 4:4, *The Amplified Bible*)

This is a very strong statement and it is surprising to some Christians. Why is our Father so emphatic in His instructions not to conform to the world's way of doing things? The answer is that the world that we live in is under the control of Satan: "...the whole world [around us] is under the power of the evil one." (I John 5:19, *The Amplified Bible*)

The more we conform to the ways of this world, the more we open the door for the one who controls the world to get at us. Satan is intelligent. He tries in every subtle way he can to tempt us into following the ways of the world. He knows this gives him an excellent opportunity to deceive us and lead us away from God's will.

Jesus Christ paid the price to crucify the world to us and us to the world: "...our Lord Jesus Christ, the Messiah, through Whom the world has been crucified to me, and I to the world!" (Galatians 6:14, *The Amplified Bible*) Our Lord wants us to be dead to this world! He doesn't want it to have any control over us. It can't have control over us if we're dead to it.

Before we were reborn spiritually, we were under the control of Satan. "Once you were under God's curse, doomed forever for your sins. You went along with the crowd and were just like all the others, full of sin, obeying Satan, the mighty prince of the power of the air, who is at work right now in the hearts of those who are against the Lord. All of us used to be just as they are..." (Ephesians 2:1-3, *The Living Bible*)

Before we were saved we went along with the world's way of doing things. Satan had a certain amount of influence over us just as he now influences people who aren't saved. Jesus rescued us from this: "He died for our sins just as God our Father planned, and rescued us from this evil world in which we live.'' (Galatians 1:4, *The Living Bible*)

In spite of the rescue that has been made available to us, many Christians still live very much as the world lives: ''If then you have died with Christ to material ways of looking at things and have escaped from the world's crude and elemental notions and teachings of externalism, why do you live as if you still belong to the world? - Why do you submit to rules and regulations?...'' (Colossians 2:20, *The Amplified Bible*)

Satan tries to tempt Christians into worldliness by doing everything he can to get us to associate regularly with unbelievers. God's Word warns us against this: ''...come out from among (unbelievers), and separate (sever) yourselves from them, says the Lord, and touch not [any] unclean thing; then I will receive you kindly and treat you with favor...'' (II Corinthians 6:17 The Amplified Bible)

If we truly seek God's will for our lives, we should be very careful about associating regularly with people who walk in spiritual darkness. I'm not saying our Father doesn't want us to witness to these people, but He doesn't want us to associate with them on a continuing basis.

It's virtually impossible to find and remain in God's will for our lives if we are in constant companionship with people who live according to the ways of the world. If we truly seek God's will, we should spend a great deal of time in fellowship with Him and in fellowship with other Christians who also seek His will with all their hearts.

We have a brand new life as Christians. It requires us to turn away from the ways of this world and to center our lives completely on the magnificence of Jesus Christ: ''...[as far as this world is concerned] you have died, and your [new, real] life is hid with Christ in God. When Christ Who is our life appears, then you also will appear with Him in (the splendor of His) glory.'' (Colossians 3:3-4, *The Amplified Bible*)

Worldly people are caught up primarily with people, places, things and events. Their values are primarily external. God's ways are very different from this. Instead of looking at us from the outside in, He looks at us from the inside out:

"...the Lord sees not as man sees; for man looks on the outward appearance, but the Lord looks on the heart." (I Samuel 16:7, *The Amplified Bible*)

He doesn't want us being preoccupied with external things. He doesn't want us trusting in, depending upon or centering our lives on the external things of this world. We should "...put no confidence or dependence [on what we are] in the flesh and on outward privileges and physical advantages and external appearances." (Philippians 3:3, *The Amplified Bible*)

The ways of this world are temporary and have no eternal value whatever: "Stop loving this evil world and all that it offers you, for when you love these things you show that you do not really love God; for all these worldly things, these evil desires - the craze for sex, the ambition to buy everything that appeals to you, and the pride that comes from wealth and importance - these are not from wealth and importance - these are not from God. They are from this evil world itself. And this world is fading away, and these evil, forbidden things will go with it, but whoever keeps doing the will of God will live forever." (I John 2:15-17, *The Living Bible*)

Our Father doesn't want us preoccupied with worldly clothing, worldly friends, worldly customs or worldly sayings. He wants us to turn away from the things of this world and to continually turn towards the eternal purpose He created us for.

Satan is very subtle. He knows how to tempt us with many things that seem to be completely harmless. Let me give you an example of this from my own life. Ever since I was a little boy I have been very interested in sports. I can remember almost fifty years ago sitting down with the sports page to go over the batting averages of all of the baseball players in minute detail.

I still follow sports today. I'm quite knowledgeable in this area and I can discuss sports with almost anyone. However, I now realize how easy it is for this to become a way of life. I see many people who are caught up with sports, hobbies and similar things that seem to be perfectly harmless.

However, some of us spend a disproportionate amount of our time in these areas.

I'm not saying that sports, hobbies and similar interests are evil. I am saying that becoming overly preoccupied with any worldly attractions can cause us to miss God's perfect will for our lives. We cannot find, enter into and remain in His perfect will if we're primarily concerned with income, homes, automobiles, vacations, sporting events, television programs, etc.

Another way Satan gets at many of us is to tempt us to be preoccupied with recognition from other human beings. Many of us spend a great deal of time and energy doing things with the primary motivation of receiving recognition from other people. God's Word warns us against this: "...am I trying to win the favor of men, or of God? Do I seek to be a man-pleaser? If I were still seeking popularity with men, I should not be a bondservant of Christ, the Messiah." (Galatians 1:10, *The Amplified Bible*)

If we are in God's will we can be assured we will be criticized by other people. The important thing is what God thinks, not what other people think. If we know we are in His will, it is very important to keep on going even though other people criticize us.

I want to balance this statement by saying that some Christians have a rebellious, maverick tendency. They never check with other people for counsel because they feel the Lord is leading them. Although we shouldn't be "man-pleasers," it's often wise to seek our pastors and elders for confirmation of God's move in our lives. This will save many of us from a lot of heartache.

We cannot find God's will if we are depending upon worldly wisdom instead of the great spiritual truth that is available to us: "Let no person deceive himself. If any one among you supposes that he is wise in this age - let him discard his [worldly] discernment and recognize himself as dull, stupid and foolish, without [true] learning and scholarship; let him become a fool that he may become [really] wise." (I Corinthians 3:18, *The Amplified Bible*)

We cannot find God's will if we are conformed to the ways of the world. Our Father is looking for children who are transformed instead of being conformed. The last part of Romans 12:2 explains this in detail.

7

Be Transformed Through A Renewed Mind

We have discussed the first portion of Romans 12:2. Before starting this chapter let's look again at this entire verse of Scripture: "Do not be conformed to this world - this age, fashioned after and adapted to its external, superficial customs. But be transformed (changed) by the [entire] renewal of your mind - by its new ideals and its new attitude - so that you may prove [for yourselves] what is the good and acceptable and perfect will of God, even the thing which is good and acceptable and perfect [in His sight for you]." (Romans 12:2, *The Amplified Bible*)

This tells us the key to turning away from the ways of this world is to be "transformed" by the renewing of our minds. The word that is translated "transformed" is the Greek word "metamorphoo." The English word "metamorphosis" which means "a complete change" comes from this word.

The same Greek word is also used in Matthew 17:2 and Mark 9:2 to describe the "transfiguration" of Jesus Christ - the total change that took place in our Lord when He went high up on a mountain with Peter, James and John. A similar complete change will take place in us if we renew our minds continually in the Word of God. This will transform our lives away from the customs of the world and enable us to experience God's perfect will.

When we are first reborn spiritually, we are still baby Christians who seek our own will: "...you are still only baby Christians, controlled by your own desires, not God's. When you are jealous of one another and divide up into quarreling groups, doesn't that prove you are still babies, wanting your own way? In fact, you are acting like people who don't belong to the Lord at all." (I Corinthians 3:3, *The Living Bible*) Some Christians never get beyond this stage. However, if we want to sincerely seek God's will for our lives we must grow spiritually. This is the only way we can overcome our natural desire to do what we want to do.

Many of us rationalize and turn things around in our minds until they seem right: "All the ways of a man are pure in his own eyes..." (Proverbs 16:2, *The Amplified Bible*) As we renew our minds continually in God's Word, we'll see the error of our ways.

Unless we renew our minds continually in God's Word, we will not be able to find His perfect will for our lives. Immature Christians cannot understand how faulty human logic can be and how useless it is in the kingdom of God: "...The Lord knows the thoughts and reasonings of the [humanly] wise and recognizes how futile they are." (I Corinthians 3:20, *The Amplified Bible*)

We aren't going to find God's perfect will unless we pay the price of developing our spiritual understanding and discernment by repeatedly renewing our minds. Satan knows this. He throws up every possible "smoke screen" to stop us from finding God's will. He wants to tempt us to do things his way. We must remember this verse: "Beloved, do not imitate evil, but imitate good. He who does good is of God; he who does evil has not seen (discerned or experienced) God - has enjoyed no vision of Him and does not know Him at all." (III John 11, *The Amplified Bible*)

It's not easy to live our lives God's way. We can only do this to the degree we are able to discern and understand God's ways because our lives have been transformed through the renewing of our minds. Satan wants us to wear "spiritual diapers" for the rest of our lives. He doesn't want us to renew our minds repeatedly to learn the way things really are in the kingdom of God.

Satan attempts to confuse us. He tries to tempt us in areas where we are weak. He tries to preoccupy us with things that have no spiritual value or importance. We are easy prey for him if we fail to grow and mature spiritually.

There is a direct ratio between spiritual maturity and fulfilling God's will for our lives. If we are well developed spiritually, we will be able to resist the temptations of Satan, our carnal nature and the ways of this world: "...stand firm and mature (in spiritual growth), convinced and fully assured in everything willed by God." (Colossians 4:12, *The Amplified Bible*)

The more we awaken spiritually, the more we will realize the complete transformation that is necessary to find God's will for our lives: "Strip yourselves of your former nature - put off and discard your old unrenewed self - which characterized your previous manner of life and becomes corrupt through lusts and desires that spring from delusion; and be constantly renewed in the spirit of your mind - having a fresh mental and spiritual attitude..." (Ephesians 4:22-23, *The Amplified Bible*)

I like The Amplified Bible's rendition of Ephesians 4:22-23. It says we must "strip ourselves" of the way we used to be. We need to throw away our old unrenewed way of doing things which was caused by delusion from Satan. The only way we can do this is to continually renew our minds in God's Word. If we do this we'll have "a fresh mental and spiritual attitude" that will light up our lives and transform them beyond our previous comprehension.

Most of us cleanse our bodies by taking a daily bath or shower. We also need to bathe ourselves continually in the purity of God's Word if we truly seek His will: "Wherewith shall a young man cleanse his way? By taking heed and keeping watch [on himself] according to Your word [conforming his life to it]. With my whole heart have I sought You, inquiring for and of You, and yearning for You; O let me not wander or step aside [either in ignorance or willfully] from Your commandments. Your word have I laid up in my heart, that I might not sin against You." (Psalm 119:9-11, *The Amplified Bible*)

The more we get into God's Word and renew our minds in it, the more we will be able to conform our lives to the instructions He has given us. The Word of God has a tremendous ability to cleanse us: "You are cleansed and pruned already, because of the Word which I have given you - the teachings I have discussed with you." (John 15:3, *The Amplified Bible*)

Our Father gave us great promises in His Word. We need to purify ourselves with them to resist anything that could stop us from entering into His will: "...since these [great] promises are ours, beloved, let us cleanse ourselves from everything that contaminates and defiles body and spirit, and bring [our] consecration to completeness in the (reverential) fear of God." (II Corinthians 7:1, *The Amplified Bible*)

God's Word is supernatural. It is perfect. It's beyond human comprehension. As we constantly renew our minds in it, it will restore everything we lost through Adam: "The law of the Lord is perfect, restoring the [whole] person..." (Psalm 19:7, *The Amplified Bible*)

Our minds are similar to computers. A computer is of no use until it is properly programmed. We must feed the right spiritual data into our minds in order to program ourselves properly to find God's will for our lives. This data comes from the Word of God. We program it into our minds by continually studying and meditating on the instructions it gives us.

The more we program God's Word deep down inside of ourselves, the better we will be to carry out His will for our lives. God's Word and His will are one and the same. As we continually program ourselves with His Word, this opens a spiritual channel to reveal more of His will for our lives.

This is a continuing process. As we grow older it becomes increasingly important to renew our minds on a daily basis: "...Though our outer man is (progressively) decaying and wasting away, yet our inner self is being (progressively) renewed day after day." (II Corinthians 4:16, *The Amplified Bible*)

This verse of Scripture has fascinated me for many years. As the years go by, our bodies progressively "decay and waste away." Our hair turns white. Many of us have to wear bifocal glasses. Our bodies show weakness in certain areas. Other signs of aging are manifested in our lives.

Our Father wants us to offset the aging process that takes place in the outer man by renewing the inner man continually! His Word tells us to renew our minds "day after day." It is vitally important for us to renew our minds daily in the Word of God. This becomes more vital as we enter into middle age and old age.

We should never stop renewing our minds. Renewal is a continuous process. It helps to dig up our old way of thinking. It helps to pull up the roots of our former way of living.

As we dig up the old roots, we plant new spiritual seeds at the same time. When we do this over a period of months and years, these new seeds develop roots of their own. These new roots are aligned with the will of God instead of the ways of this world.

This isn't easy. Satan does everything he can to stop us from renewing our minds. Our flesh rebels against continual study and meditation in the Word of God: "...much study is a weariness of the flesh." (Ecclesiastes 12:12, *The King James Bible*)

Spiritually immature people think that studying God's Word is tedious. God's ways are not the ways of the flesh. We open the door to tremendous spiritual blessings when we renew our minds continually in the Word of God. The Bible study that seems to be so tiring to the uninitiated eventually becomes very refreshing and rewarding.

Romans 12:2 says we are able to "prove" the good, acceptable and perfect will of God for our lives. God's Word is a mirror. As we renew our minds in it it reflects His will back to us. We are able to prove God's will for our lives to the degree we turn away from the customs of the world and continually renew our minds in His Word.

8

The Word Of God And The Will Of God

Our Father is able to speak to us in many ways. The most common way He speaks to His people is through His Word. The Word of God and the will of God fit together perfectly. We cannot have one without the other.

God's Word reveals His general will for our lives. As we learn and obey the general instructions our Father has given to all His children, we then will be better equipped to receive His specific instructions for our individual lives. We can't expect to find His specific will for our lives if we aren't living in obedience to His general instructions.

Our Father gave us a map - the Word of God - to show us how to stay on the general route He wants us on. His Word allows us to carefully plot our course. The obstacles along the way are clearly shown. His Word shows us how to avoid them whenever possible and how to confront them when it's not. Many of God's children wander aimlessly through life because they have not paid the price to learn and follow the directions from the map that has been provided.

Everything we need to live in conformity to the will of God has been provided for us: "Every Scripture is God-breathed - given by His inspiration - and profitable for instruction, for reproof and conviction of sin, for correction of error and discipline in obedience, and for training in righteousness [that is, in holy living, in conformity to God's will in thought, purpose and action], so that the man of God may be complete and proficient, well-fitted and thoroughly equipped for every good work." (II Timothy 3:16-17, *The Amplified Bible*)

God inspired every Scripture. Because of this it is profitable for us to learn everything we can from His Word. We then will know how to correct our mistakes and stay on track to live our lives the way He wants us to.

When we come to a crossroads and don't know which way to go, God's Word will show us. Then we can go down the correct path with complete confidence: "Thus says the Lord, Stand by the roads and look, and ask for the eternal paths, where is the good, old way; then walk in it, and you will find rest for your souls..." (Jeremiah 6:16, *The Amplified Bible*)

Our Father has given us a Book of Instructions to guide us in every area of our lives. When we obey these instructions, we will be able to escape the temptations of the world and live God's way: "...He has bestowed on us His precious and exceedingly great promises, so that through them you may escape (by flight) from the moral decay (rottenness and corruption) that is in the world because of covetousness (lust and greed), and become sharers (partakers) of the divine nature." (II Peter 1:4, *The Amplified Bible*)

Our Father knows exactly what He is talking about. Why shouldn't He? He created the world and everything in it. His Book of Instructions works! It will guide us in every area of our lives if we will follow its instructions.

God's Word is supernatural: "...the Word that God speaks is alive and full of power - making it active, operative, energizing and effective; it is sharper than any two-edged sword, penetrating to the dividing line of the breath of life (soul) and [the immortal] spirit, and of joints and marrow [that is, of the deepest parts of our nature] exposing and sifting and analyzing and judging the very thoughts and purposes of the heart." (Hebrews 4:12, *The Amplified Bible*)

God's Word is alive! It's filled with supernatural power. It contains divine energy. It is so magnificent that it is able to penetrate deep down inside of us to the very deepest parts of our being. It is able to show us what we are like deep down inside of ourselves.

It is very important for us to abide in the Word of God: "...If you abide in My Word - hold fast to My teachings and live in accordance with them - you are truly My disciples. And you will know the truth, and the truth will set you free." (John 8:31-32, *The Amplified Bible*) When we "abide" in God's Word, we live it. It becomes the center of every aspect of our lives.

When we do this we become disciples of Jesus Christ. When this happens, the supernatural truth of God's Word guides us in every area of our lives. It enables us to be set free from every way Satan tries to get at us.

God's Word will come alive in our lives if we will get in it and stay in it! However, we don't normally receive supernatural results immediately after we begin to study and meditate in the Word of God. Anyone who has studied the Bible over a period of time has found that God withholds His greatest blessings for those who persevere and patiently endure.

Many Christians aren't willing to "grind it out." Too many of us are preoccupied with the things we want to do. We don't have holy discipline. We don't have unwavering commitment. We aren't single-minded.

If we "abide" in God's Word, it will get down inside of us. It will light up our lives. It will give us great spiritual understanding. We'll realize how little we knew before: "The entrance and unfolding of Your words gives light; it gives understanding - discernment and comprehension - to the simple." (Psalm 119:130, *The Amplified Bible*)

God's Word is a lamp that shows us where to walk on the road of life. It is a light that guides us to stay on the right track: "Your word is a lamp to my feet and a light to my path." (Psalm 119:105, *The Amplified Bible*)

God's Word helps us to walk as far as we can see. When we do this in faith He will show us where to go from there: "My son, attend to my words; consent and submit to my sayings. Let them not depart from your sight; keep them in the center of your heart. For they are life to those who find them, healing and health to all their flesh. Keep your heart with all vigilance and above all that you guard, for out of it flow the springs of life." (Proverbs 4:20-23, *The Amplified Bible*)

Our Father wants us to continually study and meditate on His Word. As we do this, His supernatural Word will soar off the printed page, pierce our minds and drop down into our hearts. His Word will transform our lives if we work diligently at studying and meditating on it.

Our hearts will come alive as they are filled with the Word of God. We will have a much greater ability to conform to His will. The more we get into God's Word and the more it gets into us, the better we will know Him:

"Acquaint now yourself with Him [agree with God and show yourself to be conformed to His will] and be at peace; by that [you shall prosper and great] good shall come to you. Receive, I pray you, the law and instruction from His mouth, and lay up His words in your heart. If you return to the Almighty [and submit and humble yourself before Him], you will be built up; if you put away unrighteousness far from your tents..." (Job 22:21-23, *The Amplified Bible*)

As we humble ourselves before God and follow His instructions, He will build us up. We need to get so much of God's Word inside of us that its roots go deep into our hearts. When this happens, we will be excited about carrying out His will: "I delight to do Your will, O my God; yes, Your law is within my heart." (Psalm 40:8, *The Amplified Bible*)

The more we get into God's Word, the more we will hunger for it. We will develop an increasing love for the magnificent truth buried inside of it. Our lives will be changed beyond comprehension through its supernatural power.

Our Father gave us His Word to feed ourselves with the spiritual food we must have to carry out His will for our lives. God's Word is a love letter from our heavenly Father. It tells us everything He wants us to know to live our lives the way He wants us to live them. The more we learn from it, the more we'll want to learn.

On the other hand, if we ignore the instructions in God's Word, we are headed for problems: "Whoever despises the Word [of God] brings destruction upon himself, but he who (reverently) fears and respects the commandment [of God] shall be rewarded. The teaching of the wise is a fountain of life, that one may avoid the snares of death. Good understanding wins favor, but the way of the transgressor is hard [like the barren, dry soil or the impassable swamp]." (Proverbs 13:13-15, *The Amplified Bible*)

If we approach God's Book of Instructions with the reverent awe it deserves, we will be blessed. We will learn how to avoid the traps of spiritual death Satan sets for us. We will win favor from God.

As we study God's Word continually this will bring us into contact with the Holy Spirit. He is the Author of the Bible. He always guides us in accordance with the Holy Scriptures.

If we want to hear His still, small voice we need to study His Word continually. This tunes us in to the spiritual frequency that He speaks on. It gives Him a channel through which He can communicate with us.

The Holy Spirit lives inside of us. As we fill our minds and hearts with God's Word, this will help us to align ourselves with the Holy Spirit. This enables Him to clearly reveal God's specific will for each of our lives.

9

Guidance From The Holy Spirit

There is a definite connection between the Word of God and the Spirit of God. God's Word is truth: "...Your Word is Truth." (John 17:17, *The Amplified Bible*) The Holy Spirit also is truth. God's Word refers to Him as the Spirit of Truth:

"...when He, the Spirit of Truth (the truth-giving Spirit) comes, He will guide you into all the truth - the whole, full truth. For He will not speak His own message - on His own authority - but He will tell whatever He hears [from the Father, He will give the message that has been given to Him]..." (John 16:13, *The Amplified Bible*)

If we continually study the supernatural truth of God's Word, this will open the channel for the Spirit of Truth to guide us into His specific will for our lives. "...God has unveiled and revealed them by and through His Spirit, for the (Holy) Spirit searches diligently, exploring and examining everything, even sounding the profound and bottomless things of God - the divine counsels and things hidden and beyond man's scrutiny. For what person perceives (knows and understands) what passes through a man's thoughts except the man's own spirit within him? Just so no one discerns (comes to know and comprehend) the thoughts of God except the Spirit of God." (I Corinthians 2:10-11, *The Amplified Bible*)

The more we enter into God's will for our lives, the more we will realize our Father has given us many tasks which are beyond our ability. He does this because He wants us to be in partnership with the Holy Spirit. He never makes a mistake. He is infallible.

We make many mistakes. We can't begin to see the whole picture of God's will for our lives with our limited vision. It isn't important for us to know where we're headed as long as we know Who we are following!

The Holy Spirit has insight into great spiritual secrets because He and God are one. He will flood our hearts with spiritual understanding. This will enable us to understand exactly what He wants us to do and how He wants us to do it. If He was able to raise Jesus Christ from the dead, can't we depend on Him to guide us in His will for our lives?

He is the Master Navigator. He is fully able to chart our course through the seas of life. If we accept and follow His guidance, we'll avoid the shipwrecks and near misses all of us will encounter sooner or later when we are in control of our own lives.

The Holy Spirit knows the future. Do we? He can see many ways around our most severe problems. Can we? He will gladly take care of every detail of our lives. He is never too busy for us. He has just as much interest in the little things in our lives as He does in the seemingly big things.

Our Father doesn't want us to struggle and strain trying to carry out His will with human ability. He gave us the Holy Spirit so we can use His ability to execute His will for all of our lives. He wants us to yield our lives to His guidance: "...'Not by might, nor by power, but by my Spirit, says the Lord of Hosts...' " (Zechariah 4:6, *The Living Bible*)

There is only one way to escape the tendency to carry out our human desires: "...walk and live habitually in the (Holy)

Spirit - responsive to and controlled and guided by the Spirit; then you will certainly not gratify the cravings and desires of the flesh - of human nature without God." (Galatians 5:16, *The Amplified Bible*)

We can fulfill the Holy Spirit's will for our lives if we will let Him live His life through us. He doesn't want us to try to get Him to bless our ways. Instead, He wants us walking in continual agreement with Him. If we truly are God's children, we will gladly allow the Holy Spirit to guide us: "For all who are led by the Spirit of God are sons of God." (Romans 8:14, The Amplified Bible)

True children of God gladly give up their own desires. God the Holy Spirit lives inside of us. He gives us the desire and ability to carry out His will: "...it is God Who is all the while effectually at work in you - energizing and creating in you the power and desire - both to will and to work for His good pleasure and satisfaction and delight." (Philippians 2:13, *The Amplified Bible*)

No matter how much earthly ability we might have, He doesn't want us trying to control our lives. "...the way of a man is not in himself. It is not in man [even in a strong man and a man at his best] to direct his own steps." (Jeremiah 10:23, *The Amplified Bible*)

We can't understand His will for our lives: "Man's steps are ordered by the Lord; how can a man then understand his way?" (Proverbs 20:24, *The Amplified Bible*) The Holy Spirit can see many things we can't see. We must realize this and gladly yield control of our lives to Him.

If He's not in charge of what we're doing, we are headed for trouble. We're wasting our energy: "Except the Lord builds the house, they labor in vain who build it; except the Lord keeps the city, the watchman wakes but in vain." (Psalm 127:1, *The Amplified Bible*)

We should be ecstatic with the concept of the Holy Spirit being in complete control of every step we take in the journey of life: "The steps of a [good] man are directed and established of the Lord, when He delights in his way [and He busies Himself with his every step]." (Psalm 37:23, *The Amplified Bible*)

Satan continually tries to put thoughts into our minds. It's easy to hear Satan's voice. To fulfill God's will, we need to hear the still, small voice of the Holy Spirit. He speaks continually to all Christians, but we can't hear Him when we are preoccupied with our own desires.

We can only tune into His frequency when we give up control of our lives to Him. This enables us to hear His voice and follow His instructions: "The sheep that are My own hear and are listening to My voice, and I know them and they follow Me..." (John 10:27, *The Amplified Bible*)

He will reveal Himself to us. If we wait patiently on Him, He will speak to us telling us exactly what He wants us to do: "...your Teacher will not hide Himself any more, but your eyes shall constantly behold your Teacher. And your ears shall hear a word behind you, saying, This is the way, walk in it, when you turn to the right hand and when you turn to the left." (Isaiah 30:20-21, *The Amplified Bible*)

I can't put into words exactly how we know it is His voice. All I can say is that when we truly do yield control of our lives to Him, we will "know that we know that we know" when He speaks to us and that it is His voice we hear. We will have an absolute inner certainty of this if we dare to continually yield control of our lives to Him.

He will guide us away from the wide road of our own desires onto the narrow road of His will for our lives. Satan's ways, the ways of this world and our selfish desires are easy to find. They constitute the wide road that is easy to get on because it leads to spiritual death.

God's will for our lives is a narrow road. We can get on it and stay on it only if we are alive spiritually. We can continue on this road only when we are guided by the Holy Spirit.

If we really want to carry out God's will for our lives, we must have a continual awareness of the Holy Spirit living within us. Our consciousness of Him cannot be shallow. Every day of our lives should be focused on the magnificent One Who lives within us.

Every morning when I wake up, I start my day with a prayer something like the following: "Good morning, dear

Lord. I love You. Thank You for the fine night's sleep. Thank You for this great new day You have made. I rejoice and I'm glad in it. I yield this day totally and completely to You, Holy Spirit. Live Your life through me this day.

"Take charge of my life. Guide me every step of the way throughout this day. I don't want to do what I want to do. I want to do what You want to do, when You want to do it and how You want to do it. I willingly give up control of my life to You. Live Your wonderful life through me. I pray this in Jesus' Name. Amen."

My life has changed dramatically since I started each morning with this prayer. I can assure you the Holy Spirit wants to guide us continually throughout every day of our lives: "...the Lord shall guide you continually, and satisfy you in drought and in dry places, and make strong your bones. And you shall be like a watered garden and like a spring of water, whose waters fail not." (Isaiah 58:11, *The Amplified Bible*)

No matter how difficult the going might be, we must trust that He is there to guide us. He will bring us through the dry periods we all encounter. He will strengthen us. He will bring His will into fulfillment in our lives each and every day if we will let Him.

Do you remember how secure you felt when you were a little child walking along holding tightly onto your parents' hands? This is how it is when we allow the Holy Spirit to hold our hand and guide us throughout each day: "...I am continually with You; You do hold my right hand. You will guide me with Your counsel..." (Psalm 73:23-24, *The Amplified Bible*)

Unfortunately, many Christians go through entire days without ever once thinking of the guidance of the Holy Spirit living within them. If we seek God's will for our lives, we must realize that He lives inside of us, and He is willing and able to guide us at all times. If we turn to Him and seek His guidance, He will give us a fresh anointing each day.

He can guide us only if we surrender to Him and trust in Him. We can be filled with the Spirit only in proportion to the emptiness of our own desires. We can be guided by Him only when we give up everything else. "...I have given up everything else - I have found it to be the only way to really know Christ and to experience the mighty power that brought him back to life again..." (Philippians 3:10, *The Living Bible*)

The apostle Paul learned that we can get to know the indwelling Christ only by giving up all of our own desires. We also can experience the power and wisdom of the Holy Spirit when we surrender our desires because we sincerely want to find and carry out His will.

10

God's Will - A Little At A Time

We have seen that God's Word reveals His general plan for our lives, and the Holy Spirit reveals His specific will for our lives. However, He seldom reveals every detail at one time. I have found that He normally reveals what He wants us to do a little at a time.

During my first year as a Christian, I sought God's will continually. I set aside time every day to draw closer to Him. After I did this for sixteen months, the Holy Spirit led me to start teaching a Bible study with a group of eight people.

I spent a great deal of time preparing these Bible studies. We mimeographed them and used them as a guide for our discussion each week. In a little over a year our Bible study grew to the point where more than three hundred people were coming each Tuesday night.

After I taught for a few years the weekly studies began to accumulate into a voluminous amount of written material. Several people suggested that I write books based upon this material. Because of the anointing the Lord had given, me I believed He wanted me to do this.

I wrote a manuscript and submitted it to several Christian publishing companies. Each refused to publish it. I didn't give up. I know the Holy Spirit had led me to publish books myself. I had no idea where to begin. However, I stepped out in faith.

I spent almost every dollar I had publishing my first book, *Trust God For Your Finances.* I had twenty thousand copies printed. I took out a full-page, full-color advertisement in *The Saturday Evening Post* and several Christian magazines.

I knew nothing about publishing and distributing books. I have since learned that many authors who publish their own books end up with a large number of unsold books and stop their writing career. This didn't happen to me.

There were so many satisfied customers of *Trust God For Your Finances* that we sold many copies to people who wanted to share them with others. After our initial advertising, virtually our only method of distribution was resales to satisfied customers. Nevertheless, because this was in God's will this book had over 100,000 copies in print within five years and was translated into several foreign languages.

I was told this was an amazing record for a Christian book written by an unknown author. I was highly encouraged. I wrote and published five more Christian books. Two or three of them did fairly well, but none of them approached the record of the first book. During this time I also began to experience severe problems in several areas of my personal life.

I was amazed. What had gone wrong? Why weren't all of my books best sellers? The publishing company was doing fairly well, but why wasn't it becoming a giant?

I sought the Lord on this. The Holy Spirit gradually showed me that I had been in His will in my heart. However, when I was flushed by initial success I raced ahead of Him. I tried to do many things too quickly.

Over a period of time I have slowed down. I now realize the Lord wants me to continue to write books, but He no longer wants me to publish them. Several Christian publishers expressed interest in my books because of the initial success we experienced. I prayerfully selected a publisher. (New Leaf Press)

I then started to concentrate entirely on writing. I left the publishing to people who were much more experienced in this area than I was. Everything then started to fall into place and my writing ministry prospered.

This and similar experiences are teaching me how easy it is to get ahead of the Lord. I believe this is why He seldom reveals His will all at once. He is much, much wiser than we are. He knows how easy it is for us to get off track and to race ahead of Him.

I believe God's will is similar to pieces of a puzzle. When we buy a puzzle, there is usually a picture of the completed puzzle on the cover of the box. However, when all of the pieces are scattered on a table, it's difficult at first to see how they fit together.

When I was a child I liked to put puzzles together. I started with the outside pieces. Then I added other pieces a little at a time as I began to see how they fit together. Gradually the whole puzzle began to take shape.

I believe this is similar to the way God reveals His will to us - a little at a time: "...The God of our forefathers has destined and appointed you to come progressively to know His will - that is, to perceive, to recognize more strongly and clearly and to become better and more intimately acquainted with His will; and to see the Righteous One Jesus Christ, the Messiah and to hear a voice from His [own] mouth and a message from His [own] lips..." (Acts 22:14, *The Amplified Bible*)

This tells us that God usually reveals His will progressively. Sometimes He shows us the whole picture, but we still need to carry it out in successive steps. Each day is God's gift to us. I believe He wants us to do the best we can one day at a time without trying to rush Him in any way.

As we continually draw closer to Him, we will hear His still, small voice guiding us through each day. As I mentioned, I start each morning asking Him to reveal His will for the upcoming day. I believe the early morning hours are priceless. I have received great guidance from the Holy Spirit during this time.

Jesus apparently made a habit of getting up very early in the morning to seek His Father's will: "And in the morning, rising up a great while before day, he went out, and departed into a solitary place, and there prayed." (Mark 1:35, *The King James Bible*)

Jesus arose long before sunrise. He went off to be alone with His Father as He prayed and sought His will for the upcoming day. I believe He wants us to do likewise. He said, "...those who seek me early and diligently shall find me." (Proverbs 8:17, *The Amplified Bible*)

I believe it is very important to seek God's will each morning. Then we should wait for His guidance. "In the morning You hear my voice, O Lord; in the morning I prepare [a prayer, a sacrifice] for You, and watch and wait [for You to speak to my heart]." (Psalm 5:3, *The Amplified Bible*)

Although our Father often gives us a general picture of His will, I have found that He normally reveals His specific instructions one day at a time. He usually shows us where to put our foot when we take the next step. Then we need to step out in faith as far as we can see. If we do this He will show us the next step. If we take this He will let us see a little farther down the road.

We don't need to see far ahead. This is God's job! He has a wonderful plan for each of us. He wants us to seek this plan daily and to let Him reveal it a little at a time. As we humble ourselves before Him and seek His will throughout each day, He will lift the veil and let us see a little more.

I have found that He normally gives us small jobs when He first reveals His will to us. Do we consider these small jobs menial? Do we consider them beneath us? Or, do we do them the best we can because it is a privilege to serve Him?

Are we willing to serve our apprenticeship in seeking His will? Many of us want to "fly high" spiritually from the start. It doesn't work this way. When we seek God's will, we must be willing to start at the bottom just as we do with our secular employment.

None of us would expect to go to work for a large corporation and be in charge of the firm. It's no different in the kingdom of God. Whatever He gives us to do should be done to the best of our ability: "Whatever you do, do well..." (Ecclesiastes 9:10, *The Living Bible*)

If we aren't willing to follow God's will in the little things, He isn't going to reveal it in larger areas. Many of the great servants of God never would have achieved what they did if they hadn't been willing to do the many small jobs God gave them at the beginning. Many of us miss His will because we think the first jobs He gives us are too small and meaningless.

He knows exactly what He's doing. He knows He can't trust us to do the bigger jobs if we aren't humble enough to cheerfully do the little jobs the best we can. If we do the little jobs well, we can rest assured He will gradually move us up in His kingdom.

As this process takes place it enables us to enjoy the supernatural joy of the Lord that is reserved for those who humbly seek His will: "...You have been faithful and trustworthy over a little; I will put you in charge of much. Enter into and share the joy - the delight, the blessedness - which your master [enjoys]." (Matthew 25:23, *The Amplified Bible*)

All promotion comes from the Lord. He is the sole judge. He knows if we truly humble ourselves to seek His will. If we do, He will elevate us: "...not from the east nor from the west nor from the south come promotion and lifting up. But God is the judge! He puts down one and lifts up another." (Psalm 75:6-7, *The Amplified Bible*)

A good example of this is my oldest son. My Christian business partner and I are involved in several business ventures. The largest is a successful insurance agency which we have built over a period of thirty years. One day my partner came to me and told me he believed the Lord wanted my son, Mike, to come into our insurance business starting at the bottom as a clerk.

I thought this was all wrong. My partner was quite emphatic in saying he believed this was God's will. So I went to Mike and told him about this fully believing he wouldn't be willing to start at such a menial position. I'll never forget his reply. He said, "Don't be so sure, Dad."

Mike came to work in this lowly position. He sat out in the general office with all of the women and started at the bottom doing very menial tasks. Shortly after this, a woman who had been with us for many years in a responsible position offered her resignation without much notice. Mike was our only hope and he was thrown into this job which was far over his head. He didn't panic. He worked long and hard and never gave up even though he often was completely confused.

Over a period of time, he gradually mastered this difficult job. His performance won the respect of all our other employees. As the years progressed he willingly took on many other unpleasant jobs that no one else wanted to do. He came in early in the morning and stayed late at night.

Today he is a member of our senior staff. He didn't earn this position because he is my son. He is greatly respected by all members of our administrative staff and by all of our thirty sales representatives. He has a servant's attitude and gets great satisfaction in willingly taking on difficult jobs to help others.

I have been in the business world for more than 32 years as I write this book. Again and again I have seen people rise to great heights because they are willing to do the small things and do them right. I'm convinced that God honors people who have staying power: "...the race is not to the swift, nor the battle to the strong..." (Ecclesiastes 9:11, *The King James Bible*)

The Christian life is a marathon, not a sprint. We must be willing to start at the bottom and trust in God's ability instead of our own. We can't find His will if we are impatient. We live in an impatient age. Many of us want immediate results. God doesn't do things this way.

I believe haste comes from Satan. Satan pushes. The Holy Spirit leads. He is never in a hurry. If we trust Him we won't try to force things: "...he that believeth shall not make haste." (Isaiah 28:16, *The King James Bible*) It's a sin to rush ahead of God: "...to be over-hasty is to sin and miss the mark." (Proverbs 19:2, *The Amplified Bible*) We miss His best when we do this.

God's timing is very different from ours. He looks at everything from an eternal perspective. He has a definite time for everything in His will: "To every thing there is a season, and a time to every purpose under the heaven..." (Ecclesiastes 3:1, *The King James Bible*)

When we are in doubt I have found the best thing is to do nothing. This isn't easy to do because we feel useless. Many times God's will takes several years to come to pass. We must not get ahead of Him.

This goes against our carnal nature. Many of us feel we have to do something to help the Lord. It's very difficult to stay where we are and wait until He gives us clear instructions.

He is worth waiting for! If nothing seems to be happening, we need to patiently trust in Him: "Do not, therefore, fling away your fearless confidence, for it carries a great and glorious compensation of reward. For you have need of steadfast patience and endurance, so that you may perform and fully accomplish the will of God, and thus receive and carry away [and enjoy to the full] what is promised." (Hebrews 10:35-36, *The Amplified Bible*)

Great rewards are available to those who trust the Lord and patiently wait on Him. He will bless us in a wonderful way if we don't get ahead of Him. Good things never come easily. Many of us get a glimpse of God's will, but few are willing to pay the continual price of patiently seeking it one day at a time waiting on Him.

The will of God often requires us to deal with obstacles along the way. This is part of the grooming necessary for us to carry out His will. We must not waver:

"...my beloved brethren, be firm (steadfast), immovable, always abounding in the work of the Lord - that is, always being superior (excelling, doing more than enough) in the service of the Lord, knowing and being continually aware that your labor in the Lord is not futile - never wasted or to no purpose." (I Corinthians 15:58, *The Amplified Bible*)

This verse of Scripture tells us to be "steadfast" and "immovable" as we "abound" in God's will. The word "abound" means to be filled to the utmost with God's will. It should consume us. We should think about it constantly. The desire to find it, enter into it and carry it out should dominate our lives. This is the reason we are still here on earth.

No matter what Satan throws against us, nothing can stop us if we are in God's will: "...if this doctrine or purpose of undertaking or movement is of human origin, it will fail - be overthrown and come to nothing; but if it is of God, you will not be able to stop or overthrow or destroy them..." (Acts 5:38-39, *The Amplified Bible*)

What a magnificent promise this is! If we pursue our own goals, spiritual success is unavailable to us. However, if we are in God's will, nothing can stop us if we trust completely in Him and proceed patiently as He guides us.

We must be persistent: "...keep on seeking and you will find; keep on knocking [reverently] and the door will be opened to you." (Matthew 7:7, *The Amplified Bible*) If we persist in seeking God's will, we can claim it. If we continue to knock reverently on the door of His will, He will open it.

We can count on this. He will always do His part. Will we do ours? When everything looks dark and dreary, will we turn to Him to obtain the strength to go on? Sometimes it seems as though there is no tomorrow. When we can't see tomorrow, He can. When we can't see any way out, He can see many.

If we believe we are in His will, we must be dogged in our determination. We must not give in. No matter how intense the pressure might be, we must be very persistent in carrying out the holy assignment we have been given.

Nothing is impossible for God. All of the promises in His Word are for those who are in His will. When it seems as though we have come to a dead end, we must not stop. We should wait patiently on God knowing He will reveal the next step when He is ready.

He is looking for consistency and steadiness. If we refuse to give up and keep on going with great spiritual tenacity, He will reveal more and more of His will. Glorious rewards are availalbe to every child of God who will persist in seeking His will a little at a time refusing to give in to any obstacle.

11

Adversity And The Will Of God

If we are in the will of God, sooner or later we can expect to face adversity. Some Christians believe that everything will always go smoothly if we are in God's will. This isn't true. If it were, the apostle Paul would have been out of God's will on many occasions because he faced a lot of adversity.

What better example is there of someone in the will of God than Jesus Christ? Anyone who has read the four gospels knows He faced a great deal of adversity during His earthly ministry. He is our example in every area. It is very important to understand this when Satan whispers in our ear, "If what you are doing is in the will of God you wouldn't have all of these problems."

Some Christians believe that, if everything is going well, they must be in God's will. On the other hand, if things aren't going well, they think they aren't in God's will. This is exactly how Satan wants us to think.

It's natural to want to go through life with as much

pleasure and as little pain as possible. God's ways are quite different from ours. In His wisdom, He knows we must go through a certain amount of pain to learn what we must learn to be mature enough to carry out His will. He often allows us to go through pain for a season because He knows this is the channel for future blessings.

As we study the lives of great men and women of God, we will see they all went through difficult times. Their problems helped prepare them for God's plan for their lives. It is no different with us.

God sees far into the future. If we could see what He sees, we might not be upset with the problems we face. We would realize that overcoming our present problems will prepare us for future events we could never handle without the increased faith and endurance that comes from successfully dealing with adversity.

Some earthly parents spoil their children by trying to remove obstacles from their lives. Our heavenly Father is too wise for this. He will not hand us everything on a silver platter. He knows we need to go through fires of adversity to develop the character and maturity required to carry out His will.

He knows exactly what His plans are for each of us. He can see very clearly the areas in our lives that must be changed before we can carry out these plans. He knows how beautiful our lives will be if we are broken in these areas.

If we seek His will, we are often required to suffer unjustly: "...[it is] better to suffer [unjustly] for doing right, if that should be God's will, than to suffer [justly] for doing wrong." (I Peter 3:17, *The Amplified Bible*)

Sometimes it is good for us to suffer even though we do nothing wrong. This has happened to me. I don't want to write about the details because it is so personal. I have gone to God many times and said, "Why did this happen to me? It isn't fair. I never did anything to deserve this."

If we seek God's will, sometimes we're going to have to put up with things that "aren't fair." Satan isn't fair. If we sincerely seek God's will, Satan is going to try to bring adversity upon us.

If we're in God's will, we can expect to be persecuted by others: "Indeed all who delight in piety and are determined to live a devoted and godly life in Christ Jesus will meet with persecution - that is, will be made to suffer because of their religious stand." (II Timothy 3:12, *The Amplified Bible*)

It's important to notice the word "all" in this verse of Scripture. This doesn't say that some Christians who are determined to seek God's will are going to meet with persecution. It says all of us will!

Satan hates to see Christians who are determined to seek God's will. One of his most effective techniques is to influence the minds of others to cause them to persecute us. Sometimes members of our families will turn against us because of our strong conviction to carry out God's will: "...a man's foes will be they of his own household." (Matthew 10:36, *The Amplified Bible*)

It's not uncommon for our brothers and sisters to turn against us when we are in the will of God. It's not uncommon for children to turn against parents or parents to turn against children. Sometimes one spouse even turns against the other. Members of my family have turned against me because of my strong commitment to carry out God's will.

We also can expect to be persecuted by unsaved people: "If you belonged to the world, the world would treat you with affection and would love you as its own. But because you are not of the world - are no longer one with it - but I have chosen (selected) you out of the world, the world hates (detests) you." (John 15:19, *The Amplified Bible*)

When we ardently pursue God's will, our lifestyle is much different from the way the world lives. Many unsaved people who observe us feel threatened. If what we are doing is right, their standard of values is wrong.

This is why we can expect some people to disagree when we pursue God's will. It shouldn't take us unaware: "Do not be surprised and wonder, brethren, that the world detests and pursues you with hatred." (I John 3:13, *The Amplified Bible*)

The more worldly people are, the more they will disagree if our lifestyle is vastly different from theirs. They can't understand God's ways. His ways are so different from the world's ways that some people will think we have "gone off the deep end" when we are actually in the center of God's will.

If we are going to live a Godly life in the midst of an ungodly world, we can't expect carnal people to understand. They walk to a different drumbeat. They serve a different master. They have no perception of spiritual things.

If they persecute us, we should rejoice: "Blessed - happy [with life-joy and satisfaction in God's favor and salvation, apart from your outward condition] and to be envied - are you when people despise (hate) you, and when they exclude and excommunicate you (as disreputable), and revile and denounce you, and defame and cast out and spurn your name as evil (wicked) on account of the Son of man. Rejoice and be glad at such a time, and exult and leap for joy, for behold, your reward is rich and great and strong and intense and abundant in heaven; for even so their forefathers treated the prophets." (Luke 6:22-23, *The Amplified Bible*)

When we seek God's will, we must not fall into the trap of judging everything based upon the short period of time we live on earth. When we get to heaven, many of us will receive great eternal rewards for the persecution we go through. We will meet many others in heaven who have been persecuted because they sought God's will.

Sometimes God uses adversity to mold our character: "...For who can resist and withstand His will? But who are you, a mere man, to criticize and contradict and answer back to God? Will what is formed say to him that formed it, Why have you made me thus? Has the potter no right over the clay, to make out of the same mass (lump) one vessel for beauty and distinction and honorable use, and another for menial or ignoble and dishonorable use?" (Romans 9:19-21, *The Amplified Bible*)

We are the clay and God is the Potter. He knows exactly what He's doing when He molds us: "Woe to the man who fights with his Creator. Does the pot argue with its maker? Does the clay dispute with him who forms it, saying, 'Stop, you're doing it wrong!' or the pot exclaim, 'How clumsy can you be!'?" (Isaiah 45:9, *The Living Bible*)

We must trust God. Many things that hurt us deeply actually purify us and correct us from the error of our ways: "Blows that wound cleanse away evil, and strokes [for correction] reach to the innermost parts." (Proverbs 20:30, *The Amplified Bible*)

If we are going through difficult times as a result of seeking God's will, we can trust Him. He will never let us down: "...those who are ill-treated and suffer in accordance with God's will must do right, and commit their souls (in charge as a deposit) to the One Who created them and will never fail [them]." (I Peter 4:19, *The Amplified Bible*)

We must be willing to go through the fire. If we seek God's will, we must expect to be cleansed. Our impurities need to be removed. They aren't removed during easy times.

Jesus suffered. If we earnestly seek God's will, we will suffer too: "...since Christ suffered in the flesh [for us, for you], arm yourselves with the same thought and purpose [patiently to suffer rather than fail to please God]. For whoever has suffered in the flesh [having the mind of Christ] has done with [intentional] sin - has stopped pleasing himself and the world, and pleases God." (I Peter 4:1-2, *The Amplified Bible*)

Our goal should be to please God, not ourselves. Sometimes He allows Satan to do things to us that seem bad. However, God in His wisdom is able to make all of our problems work together for good if we react to them the way His Word tells us to react.

If we could see things the way He sees them, we wouldn't complain. If we could see the end result as He does, we would be patient. Many times doors that seem closed actually open unto a new and different road - a road we couldn't get on if we hadn't come upon the door seemingly closed by adversity.

God is fully capable of turning the attacks of Satan into good: "And after you have suffered a little while, the God of all grace - Who imparts all blessing and favor - Who has called you to His [own] eternal glory in Christ Jesus, will

Himself complete and make you what you ought to be, establish and ground you securely, and strengthen (and settle) you." (I Peter 5:10, *The Amplified Bible*)

If we diligently seek God's will, His wonderful grace will be with us as we travel through challenges. If we react to adversity as His Word instructs us He will bring us out on the other side full and complete. His grace is more than sufficient.

He will never withhold blessings from His children who are living according to His will. If we seek His will and if we understand the spiritual truths explained here, we will experience His supernatural peace as we go through adversity. We'll know deep down inside of ourselves that He is in complete control and that everything will work out very well if we continue to trust completely in Him.

12

Faith And The Will Of God

If we believe with all our hearts that we are in the will of God, we can rely on Him to bring us through any adversity we face. He wants us to use the same faith we used to be reborn spiritually to deal with our problems.

If we can trust Him to get us to heaven, we certainly can trust Him to guide us daily as we do our best to carry out His will here on earth: "...just as you trusted Christ to save you, trust Him, too, for each day's problems; live in vital union with Him. Let your roots grow down into Him and draw up nourishment from Him." (Colossians 2:6-7, *The Living Bible*)

If we really want to carry out God's will, we must continually draw closer to Him. We need to spend precious time each day building our faith through Bible study, meditation, prayer, worship, fellowship with other Christians and, above all else, fellowship with Him.

As we do this the roots of our faith will grow deeper. Fear won't be able to get at us: "You shall establish yourself on righteousness - right, in conformity with God's will and order; you shall be far even from the thought of oppression or destruction, for you shall not fear; and from terror, for it shall not come near you." (Isaiah 54:14, *The Amplified Bible*)

If we wholeheartedly seek God's will and do our very best to get in it and stay in it, we have nothing to fear. He is completely capable of handling every problem we will face. If we know we are in God's will, we have every right to believe He will bring us safely through every problem.

We cannot be defeated because the will of God cannot be defeated. The variables are the strength of our faith, our endurance and our perseverance. The will of God will always prevail if our faith does not break down.

The safest place we can be is in the center of God's will. Spiritual security comes from finding His will, doing our best to stay in it and trusting continuously in Him. Satan cannot defeat us if we follow these instructions.

No matter how difficult our problems might be, we must not back off. If we are in God's will, it is His responsibility to pull us through. We must fulfill our responsibility to trust Him completely and not to give up no matter how difficult our problems might seem to be.

He will do His part. Will we do ours? Will our faith be strong enough? Will it endure? "...I have set my face like flint to do His will, and I know that I will triumph." (Isaiah 50:7, *The Living Bible*)

Flint is an extremely hard rock which is common in Palestine, Syria and Egypt. This fine-grained siliceous rock is so hard that it produces sparks when it is struck with steel. It is a symbol of hardness because it is unyielding.

This is how our Father wants us to live when we earnestly seek His will. If we do this we will share in Christ's victory. We will not be denied just as He refused to be denied.

A heart filled with the desire to do God's will is able to appropriate the promises of His Word with confident faith. This is why God put these promises in His Word! They aren't for people who are carrying out their own will. They are for

God's children who are in His will.

Our father didn't give us faith to see our selfish desires accomplished. He gave us faith so we could use it to carry out His will. The more we are in His will, the better our faith will work.

He can solve every problem. When we are in His will, we should refuse to focus on the problems we face. Instead, we should focus continuously upon the Lord, trusting in Him with the faith of a little child.

Job was in God's will. He faced seemingly insurmountable problems, but he knew God could solve every problem. He knew God's will could not be stopped: "I know you can do anything and that no one can stop you." (Job 42:2, *The Amplified Bible*)

When we face difficult problems as we seek God's will, we need the same kind of faith Job had. We should turn humbly to God with complete trust just as sheep humbly follow their shepherd knowing he will bring them to safety. We have every right to expect our Shepherd to protect us. He is victorious: "...All authority - all power of rule - in heaven and on earth has been given to Me." (Matthew 28:18, *The Amplifield Bible*)

He is Almighty God, not "part mighty God." His power is absolute. Nothing can stop Him. No matter what we are faced with, He will bring us safely through if we will trust Him and keep on trusting no matter how long it takes.

He cannot lose. He wins every time. We cannot lose if we are in His will, if we keep building our faith and if we endure and persevere for as long as we have to.

He wants us to dare to let go of our problems. He wants us to give them to Him because we trust completely in Him: "Roll your works upon the Lord - commit and trust them wholly to Him; [He will cause your thoughts to become agreeable to His will, and] so shall your plans be established and succeed." (Proverbs 16:3, *The Amplified Bible*)

Our part is to give our problems to Him and to refuse to take them back. If we do this, He will cause our goals to stay in harmony with His will, and He will bring us through to success.

Moses was in God's will when he came to the Red Sea. He didn't know how to cross this body of water, but he knew how to trust God to solve the problem. God parted the waters for him.

Jesus was in the will of God when He faced thousands of people with no apparent way to feed them. He trusted completely in His Father. God honored His faith and provided more than enough food.

Shadrach, Meshach and Abednego were in the will of God. Even though they were placed in a fiery furnace with no apparent way of escape, they dared to trust God. He brought them safely through.

God doesn't change: "...I am the Lord, I change not..." (Malachi 3:6, *The King James Bible*) If we're doing our very best to carry out His will, we have every right to trust Him to handle every problem just as Moses, Jesus, Shadrach, Meshach and Abednego trusted Him.

Do we really believe He will take care of every problem? Do we dare to let go? "Cast your burden on the Lord [releasing the weight of it] and He will sustain you; He will never allow the [consistently] righteous to be moved - made to slip, fall or fail." (Psalms 55:22, *The Amplified Bible*)

I believe the words "consistently righteous" are important. If we're consistently righteous, we are continuously doing our best to live our lives the way God wants us to live them. This is what we do when we seek His will at all times.

If we do this we have every right to cast the weight of our problems on Him. He won't let us down. We don't need to carry burdens that are too heavy for us. Our Lord never meant us to do this. They are His problems, not ours.

"Come to Me, all you who labor and are heavy-laden and over burdened, and I will cause you to rest - I will ease and relieve and refresh your souls. Take My yoke upon you, and learn of Me; for I am gentle (meek) and humble (lowly) in heart, and you will find rest - relief, ease and refreshment and recreation and blessed quiet - for your souls. For My yoke is wholesome (useful, good) - not harsh, hard, sharp or pressing, but comfortable, gracious and pleasant; and My burden is light and easy to be borne." (Matthew 11:28-30, *The Amplified Bible*)

This is one reason it's such a joy to be in God's will. We don't have to carry heavy loads. Jesus told us to give them to Him. He said He would cause us to rest and be refreshed.

How do we enter into His rest? We do this by taking His yoke upon us. A yoke is a wooden frame used to fit a pair of animals together. It is often used to control a pair of oxen.

They have no freedom of movement when they have a yoke around their necks. They're locked in place. They are controlled by the yoke. They have to do exactly what the person in the driver's seat wants them to do.

Jesus will take care of our heavy loads if we will get into His yoke! Instead of struggling and straining trying to carry these loads ourselves, He wants us to humble ourselves before Him. He wants us to willingly give up control of our lives, trusting completely in Him to guide us.

When we are in His will, we're similar to oxen in a yoke. We're humble and lowly. We're completely under the control of Jesus just as the oxen are completely under the control of the person in the driver's seat.

If Jesus really is in control, we will be able to remain calm no matter what we face. We can enter into His rest because we know we are doing what He wants us to do. No problem is too great for Him: "I have strength for all things in Christ Who empowers me - I am ready for anything and equal to anything through Him Who infuses inner strength into me, [that is, I am self-sufficient in Christ's sufficiency.]" (Philippians 4:13, *The Amplified Bible*)

His strength is more than sufficient. We can handle anything we face if we seek His will and if we dare to give complete control of our lives to Him. If we do this, He will exchange His strength for our weakness. This is how we use faith to carry out His will for our lives.

13

Prayer And The Will Of God

I believe the primary reason God has given us faith is to use it in our prayers. However, He didn't give us the ability to pray in faith so that we can pray for requests that are not in His will.

We're wasting our time when we pray according to our will instead of praying according to God's will: "...you do ask [God for them] and yet fail to receive, because you ask with wrong purpose and evil, selfish motives. Your intention is, [when you get what you desire] to spend it in sensual pleasures." (James 4:3, *The Amplified Bible*)

When we pray like this, whether we realize it or not, we're asking God to answer sinful prayer requests. All sin is based upon five words - "I'll do it my way." This is evil in God's eyes: "...he did evil, for he did not set his heart to seek (inquire of, yearn for) the Lord with all his desire." (II Chronicles 12:14, *The Amplified Bible*)

How can we expect a pure, sinless God to accept a sinful prayer? On the other hand, we can approach Him with strong, unwavering faith when we know we pray for something in His will: "...beloved, if our consciences (our hearts) do not accuse us - if they do not make us feel guilty and condemn us - we have confidence (complete assurance and boldness) before God; and we receive from Him whatever we ask for, because we (watchfully) obey His orders - observe His suggestions and injunctions, follow His plan for us - and (habitually) practice what is pleasing to Him." (I John 3:21-22, *The Amplified Bible*)

If we have a clear conscience about our prayer requests, we won't feel guilty when we pray. We'll be able to pray with confidence. We'll know God will answer because we are doing our very best to live our lives the way He wants.

This verse of Scripture ties in perfectly with my two favorite verses of Scripture on the subject of prayer - I John 5:14-15. Here is the first one: "And this is the confidence - the assurance, the [privilege of] boldness - which we have in Him: [we are sure] that if we ask anything (make any request) according to His will (in agreement with His own plan) He listens to and hears us." (I John 5:14, *The Amplified Bible*)

Can you imagine yourself picking up the telephone to call the President of the United States any time during the day or night with the absolute certainty that you could get through to him? As preposterous as this might seem, the truth is that we can get through to One Who is much greater than the President of the United States any time we pray according to His will.

All Christians have the supernatural ability to contact the Creator of the universe at any time. We can be absolutely certain that He will always listen to our requests. He is never too busy to hear us. He listens to everything we say - unless our prayer isn't in His will: "If I regard iniquity in my heart, the Lord will not hear me..." (Psalm 66:18, *The King James Bible*)

Iniquity means sin. If our prayers are for selfish desires, God doesn't hear our requests. When we do pray according to His will, Jesus Christ - Who conforms to His Father's will in every way - intercedes for us: "...we have an Advocate

(One Who will intercede for us) with the Father; [it is] Jesus Christ [the all] righteous - upright, just, Who conforms to the Father's will in every purpose, thought and action." (I John 2:1, *The Amplified Bible*)

An advocate is like a lawyer who represents us to someone else. When we pray according to God's will, Jesus represents us to God. He does this continually: "...He is always living to make petition to God and intercede with Him and intervene for them." (Hebrews 7:25, *The Amplified Bible*)

Jesus sits at God's right hand to intercede when we pray according to His will. Isn't it wonderful to know we can approach God at any time and know that He hears us as Jesus intercedes for us?

We have absolute certainty that God hears us. The second of my favorite Scripture verses on prayer says we are certain He will answer each and every prayer request according to His will: "And if (since) we [positively] know that He listens to us in whatever we ask, we also know [with settled and absolute knowledge] that we have [granted us as our present possessions] the requests made of Him." (I John 5:15, *The Amplified Bible*)

This is amazing! It may sound too good to be true, but God's Word says we can be certain He carefully listens to each prayer request made according to His will. We can also be certain He answers every one of these requests. Do you think these last two sentences are an exaggeration? Go back and study I John 5:14-15 carefully and see for yourself.

God doesn't answer prayers according to His will some of the time or most of the time. He answers every one. George Mueller, one of the greatest saints who ever lived, said he never brought one prayer request to God that wasn't answered. However, some of them took a long time - sometimes as long as thirty or forty years.

God will answer every prayer made according to His will if our faith is strong enough and if we endure long enough. Jesus explained this when He said, "...whatever you ask for in prayer, having faith and [really] believing, you will receive." (Matthew 21:22, *The Amplified Bible*)

We shouldn't think this is too good to be true. This is why God created prayer. This is why He created faith. He gave us prayer as a channel to come to Him with requests according to His will. He gave us faith so we could dare to trust Him to do exactly what His Word says He will do.

Unfortunately, many of us don't pray according to His will. Some of us pray according to His will, but our faith is not strong enough. Others pray according to His will with strong faith, but we don't endure long enough.

Nothing lies beyond the reach of prayer except requests made outside the will of God, requests made without sufficient faith or requests made without patient, enduring persistence. God's delay is not God's denial. If we pray according to His will, if our faith is strong and if we persist and refuse to give up, we will receive the answer!

Some Christians will disagree with what I have written in the last several paragraphs. They don't believe God will answer every prayer request made according to His will. They should go back and carefully study the verses of Scripture in this chapter. I have not exaggerated.

Too many of us limit God when there is absolutely nothing He will not do for us if our prayers are according to His will. We then must add faith and endurance to receive this answer: "...through faith [that is, by their leaning of the entire personality on God in Christ in absolute trust and confidence in His power, wisdom and goodness], and by practice of patient endurance and waiting are [now] inheriting the promises." (Hebrews 5:12, *The Amplified Bible*)

I like the amplification of the word "faith." We are told this means "to lean our entire personality on God in Christ in absolute trust and confidence in His power, wisdom and goodness." If we do this and then patiently endure while we wait for His perfect timing to bring the answer into manifestation, we will receive the answer.

This doesn't just apply to our "big" prayer requests. God's will includes every area. It includes the little things as well as the big things. Our heavenly Father is interested in the little things in our lives just as earthly parents are interested in the little things in their children's lives.

We all have to make a continual series of decisions. Our Father wants us to come to Him in prayer continually: "Be unceasing in prayer - praying perseveringly..." (I Thessalonians 5:17, *The Amplified Bible*)

This is what I do. I start each morning with prayer. I pray at the end of each day. I also pray many times throughout the day. I never write one word in any of my books without praying first to ask the Holy Spirit to guide and anoint my writing. Before each business appointment, I pray for guidance. I never attempt to counsel anyone without first praying for wisdom.

I seldom make a purchase without first asking for the Lord's guidance. I go to Him on many occasions during each day to ask Him to show me what decision to make. I know how helpless I am and how often I need His help throughout each day of my life.

Too many of us make decisions based upon what we think is right. Then we ask our Father to bless these decisions. This is wrong. We should never make a decision without first seeking His guidance.

He has given us the Holy Spirit to live within us to guide us throughout each day of our lives. We should never make a decision until we are at peace deep down inside of ourselves. If we don't have peace, we should either say "no" or keep waiting until we have peace.

Satan wants us to impulsively do whatever we want to do. The Holy Spirit wants us to wait patiently until He gives us the peace we are doing the right thing. We must not give in to Satan. We must wait patiently until the Holy Spirit allows us to proceed.

Each time we stop to seek God's will, it becomes easier to do this in the future. Eventually, it becomes a way of life to prayerfully seek His will on many occasions throughout each day. This is why we were given the privilege of prayer.

14

True Fulfillment

Deep down inside of ourselves we all crave fulfillment. We have a strong desire for satisfaction. We want our lives to have meaning. We don't want to live empty lives.

However, we will never experience true fulfillment unless we find God's will for our lives, enter into it and remain in it. We will never have an inner sense of completeness unless we are successfully carrying out the assignments He has given us.

Satan knows nothing is more meaningful and fulfilling than carrying out God's will. He also knows nothing is more empty and futile than carrying out our own will. He does everything he can to deceive us into seeking our will or falling for the temptations he dangles in front of us.

He was able to tempt Adam and Eve to turn from God's will. His goal hasn't changed. He'll do anything he can to tempt us to turn away from God's will and towards self-will.

One of his most effective techniques is to tempt us to seek pleasure. Some people devote their lives to seeking pleasure. People who fall into this trap are spiritually poor: "He who loves pleasure will be a poor man..." (Proverbs 21:17, *The Amplified Bible*)

It's foolish to chase after pleasure. Jesus told us this when He spoke of a rich man who had decided to lay up treasure so he could live a life of ease: "...I will say to my soul, Soul, you have many good things laid up, [enough] for many years; take your ease, eat, drink and enjoy yourself merrily. But God said to him, You fool!..." (Luke 12:19-20, *The Amplified Bible*)

We'll never find meaning and fulfillment through the things of this world. If we seek satisfaction through our five senses, we delude ourselves: "...the eye is not satisfied with seeing, nor the ear filled with hearing." (Ecclesiastes 1:8, *The Amplified Bible*)

Satan wants us chasing after worldly goals because he knows "...the lust of the eyes of man is never satisfied." (Proverbs 27:20, *The Amplified Bible*) Worldly goals, possessions or accomplishments only give temporary satisfaction. Soon after we receive them, we are looking for something else.

A sinful life is a life spent chasing after personal desires. God's Word tells us we only receive temporary enjoyment from this. It speaks of the "...fleeting enjoyment of a sinful life." (Hebrews 11:25, *The Amplified Bible*)

Jesus Christ is the only One Who can satisfy our spiritual hunger and thirst: "...I am the Bread of Life. He who comes to Me will never be hungry and he who believes on and cleaves to and trusts in and relies on Me will never thirst any more - at any time." (John 6:35, *The Amplified Bible*)

We will experience complete satisfaction only if we hunger and thirst after God's will: "Blessed and fortunate and happy and spiritually prosperous [that is, in that state in which the born-again child of God enjoys His favor and salvation] are those who hunger and thirst for righteousness (uprightness and right standing with God), for they shall be completely satisfied!" (Matthew 5:6, *The Amplified Bible*)

We can't satisfy our deep inner thirst by achieving personal goals. This can be satisfied only through the living water of the Holy Spirit's will for our lives: "...If any man is thirsty, let him come to Me and drink! He who believes in Me - who cleaves to and trusts in and relies on Me - as the Scripture has said, Out from his innermost being springs and rivers of living water shall flow (continuously)." (John 7:37-38, *The Amplified Bible*)

We're foolish to do what we want to do. This will inevitably lead us down the path of spiritual death and emptiness: "There is a way that seems right to a man and appears straight before him, but at the end of it are the ways of death." (Proverbs 16:25, *The Amplified Bible*)

There is only one way to find true meaning and fulfillment. We will never truly be fulfilled unless we willingly and cheerfully surrender our lives to do what the Lord wants us to do with them: "...Only those who throw away their lives for My sake and for the sake of the Good News will ever know what it means to really live." (Mark 8:35, *The Living Bible*)

Very few people understand that the only way to find deep inner meaning and fulfillment is to give up control of our lives. Before we became Christians, we were children of Satan, and our primary goal was to please ourselves. After we become Christians, we are children of God, and our primary goal should be to please Him.

Before we became Christians, we found brief periods of what seemed like happiness from doing what we wanted to do. After we become Christians, real meaning and fulfillment can come only from doing what the Lord wants us to do. This is why Jesus died for us: "...He died for all, so that all those who live might live no longer to and for themselves, but to and for Him Who died and was raised again for their sake." (II Corinthians 5:15, *The Amplified Bible*)

There is only one thing that will cause our souls to come alive. This is to turn continually to the Holy Spirit within us and to follow His guidance to the best of our ability: "Incline your ear [submit and consent to the Divine will], and come to Me; hear, and your soul shall revive..." (Isaiah 55:3, *The Amplified Bible*)

He will show us the path He has for us. As we continuously draw closer to Him and follow this path, He will fill our lives with joy and guide us to eternal pleasure: "You will show me the path of life; in Your presence is fullness of joy, at Your right hand there are pleasures for evermore." (Psalms 16:11, *The Amplified Bible*)

It is vitally important to realize how useless our plans are. We were created for a specific purpose, and we will experience the fulfillment the Lord has for us only when we achieve this: "Many plans are in a man's mind, but it is the Lord's purpose for him that will stand." (Proverbs 19:21, *The Amplified Bible*)

Our Father would never ask us to give up our personal plans and dreams without offering us something much better - His plan for our lives. We must not get caught up with our plans: "Look here, you people who say, 'Today or tomorrow we are going to such and such a town, stay there a year, and open up a profitable business.' How do you know what is going to happen tomorrow? For the length of your lives is as uncertain as the morning fog - now you see it; soon it is gone. What you ought to say is, 'If the Lord wants us to, we shall live and do this or that.' " (James 5:13-15, *The Living Bible*)

We don't know what the future holds. Our lives are temporary and uncertain. We must turn away from our goals to seek the Lord's will at all times.

How can we possibly choose anything better than His goals for us? It's foolish to assume our goals could be as good as His goals. We can't even begin to see the things He can see. His way is the only way.

He knows exactly what it takes to fulfill us. He created us and He knows each of us intimately. We must not try to fulfill ourselves. Our goals and desires will always cause us to come up empty.

I believe God put His will inside of us before we were born. I believe it is programmed deep down inside of each of us. The more we seek His will, the more we'll know this is "it" when we find it.

When God created us, He created a vacuum on the inside of us. Nothing can fill this except to find and carry out the purpose we were created for. Only God can satisfy the craving of our souls: "...He satisfies the longing soul, and fills the hungry soul with good." (Psalms 107:9, *The Amplified Bible)*

In recent years, a great deal has been written about mid-life crisis. When we're in our teens, twenties and thirties, chasing after pleasure can give us a fairly enjoyable life. However, as we grow older, we find our lives becoming increasingly empty if we continue to chase pleasure and seek personal goals.

It's very common for people to raise a family, accumulate considerable worldly possessions and wonder why they feel so empty when they finally have everything they have striven after for many years. They think, "There has to be more to life than this." This is what mid-life crisis is all about.

Mid-life crisis comes when we realize we are in the last half of our lives and feel very empty deep down inside. I believe all mid-life crisis has its roots in many years of pursuing our own will and can only be solved by completely abandoning this and continually seeking God's will.

Unfortunately, many people who are faced with mid-life crisis do exactly the opposite. Because they feel so empty inside, they explode into a frenzy of activity chasing after new goals.

This is exactly how Satan wants frustrated people to react to mid-life crisis. He wants them to try to fill the aching void within them through other people, places, things and events. He knows we cannot find the solution to mid-life crisis in the world and he's delighted if we try to do this.

God's ways are vastly different from ours. The reason people experience mid-life crisis in the first place is because the vacuum He created within them remains unfilled. They can only fill this by realizing their spiritual emptiness and forsaking everything else so they can seek His will.

It's never too late. Even though many of us have sinned by doing things our way for a long time, we can repent, ask our Father's forgiveness and devote the rest of our lives to seeking His will.

All Christians will experience fulfillment in heaven because every person in heaven submits completely to God's will. As we grow older we can enjoy a preview of heaven and escape the emptiness of mid-life crisis by turning away from our own desires.

The apostle Paul was a great man of God. His life was filled with great spiritual achievements. However, none of these things impressed him: "...none of these things move me; neither do I esteem my life dear to myself, if only I may finish my course with joy, and the ministry which I have obtained of [entrusted to me by] the Lord Jesus, faithfully to attest the good news (Gospel) of God's grace - His unmerited favor, spiritual blessing and mercy." (Acts 20:24, *The Amplified Bible*)

As Paul approached the end of his life, he had only one goal - to finish his life filled with joy because he was successfully accomplishing the ministry Jesus had given him. We should have this same goal.

As the years of our lives wind down to a precious few, it becomes increasingly important to turn away from our personal desires. It's never too late to experience true fulfillment that is available if we cheerfully turn away from everything except seeking God's will.

15

The Blessings Of Obedience

In the previous fourteen chapters I have outlined all of the Scriptural instructions I could find in regard to God's will for our lives. In this final chapter we'll look at the blessings we will receive if we obey these instructions.

God is bound by His laws. His Word says He is no respecter of persons. He wants to bless all His children, but His Word says He resists the proud. We block His blessings if we insist on carrying out our own will. We open the door to these blessings by continually seeking His will.

Nothing makes our Father happier than to see us continually seeking His will. Think how happy human parents would be if their adult children regularly came to them for advice and then followed this advice. Our heavenly Father is no different. We make Him very happy when we continually seek His will.

Love and obedience go together. If we truly love someone, we want to please him. We show how much we really love our Father by our obedience: "...The [true] love of God is this, that we do His commands - keep His ordinances and are mindful of His precepts and teaching..." (I John 5:3, *The Amplified Bible*)

When His will means more to us than anything else and we seek it with all our hearts, this opens the door for Him to pour out blessings upon us: "Blessed, happy, fortunate [to be envied] are they who keep His testimonies, and who seek, inquire for and of Him and crave Him with the whole heart." (Psalms 119:2, *The Amplified Bible*)

Our Father blesses His plans, not ours. If we do our very best to submit to Him and carry out His desires, He will reward us: "If they obey and serve him, they shall spend their days in prosperity, and their years in pleasures." (Job 36:11, *The King James Bible*)

All Christians want to receive blessings from God. We receive these blessings by giving up our way of doing things and continually seeking His will. When we follow His instructions, we open the door to many benefits: "...No good thing will He withhold from those who walk uprightly." (Psalms 84:11, *The Amplified Bible*)

Our Father won't withhold any blessings from us if we always do our best to walk in obedience to Him. Too many of us ask Him to bless us when we do what we want to do. His best blessings are reserved for His children who humble themselves before Him and yield completely to His will.

None of us deserve blessings from God. Nevertheless, He will give us many blessings if we continually turn away from our desires and humbly seek His will: "...He gives his undeserved favor to the low [in rank], the humble and the afflicted." (Proverbs 3:34, *The Amplified Bible*)

God will bless us in a wonderful way during our lives on earth when we conform to His will. However, this pales in significance to the blessings that will be reserved for us when we arrive in heaven.

It's easy to look at things from an earthly perspective instead of an eternal perspective. Some of us tend to place too much emphasis on the seventy, eighty or ninety years we expect to spend on this earth. We're going to live in heaven much, much longer than we live on earth.

God created each of us to fulfill a specific assignment while we are here on earth. We must not be blinded by our carnal desires during the relatively short number of years we spend here. Instead, we should always strive to see things from His eternal perspective.

Satan hates to see us looking at things from an eternal perspective. He knows full well that he is going to spend eternity in "...the fiery lake of burning brimstone..." where he "...will be tormented day and night forever and ever - through the ages of the ages." (Revelation 20:10, *The Amplified Bible*) He wants us to suffer with him eternally.

If we are reborn spiritually, his next goal is to do everything he can to get us to miss God's will during our lives on earth. He wants us to get all caught up with worldly goals. He doesn't want us to have an eternal perspective.

The apostle Paul looked at his life from an eternal perspective as he approached death: "...I am already about to be sacrificed - my life is about to be poured out [as a drink offering]; the time of my [spirit's] release [from the body] is at hand and I will soon go free. I have fought the good (worthy, honorable and noble) fight; I have finished the race; I have kept (firmly held) the faith. (As to what remains,) henceforth there is laid up for me the [victor's] crown of righteousness - for being right with God and doing right - which the Lord, the righteous Judge, will award to me and recompense me on that [great] day; and not to me only but also to all those who have loved and yearned for and welcomed His appearing [His return]." (II Timothy 4:6-8, *The Amplified Bible*)

Paul knew he had been successful in carrying out God's will. He knew great rewards awaited him in heaven. Similar rewards are available to all of God's children who successfully carry out His will.

Our real home is in heaven. One day we will be judged there in regard to how well we carried out our assignments here on earth: "...we must all appear and be revealed as we are before the judgment seat of Christ, so that each one may receive [his pay] according to what he has done in the body, whether good or evil, [considering what his purpose and motive have been, and what he has achieved, been busy with and given himself and his attention to accomplishing]." (II Corinthians 5:10, *The Amplified Bible*)

When we get to heaven, the results of our lives on earth will be very obvious: "The work of each [one] will become (plainly, openly) known - shown for what it is; for the day (of Christ) will disclose and declare it, because it will be revealed with fire, and the fire will test and critically appraise the character and worth of the work each person has done. If the work which any person has built on this Foundation - any product of his efforts whatever - survives (this test), he will get his reward. But if any person's work is burned up [under the test], he will suffer the loss (of it all, losing his reward), though he himself will be saved, but only as [one who has passed] through fire." (I Corinthians 3:13-15, *The Amplified Bible*)

If the Lord's evaluation of our lives shows we did carry out His will we will be rewarded. If we miss His will, we will still live eternally in heaven, but we will miss out on the glorious rewards we could have received.

The Lord has blessings beyond our fondest dreams to bestow upon those who leave all to follow Him. The temptations of this world are nothing compared to the magnificent eternal blessings available to Christians who turned away from everything else to carry out His will.

When we get to heaven I believe special rewards will be given to God's children who cheerfully did things they didn't want to do because they knew this was His will. I believe the eternal leaders in the kingdom of heaven will be chosen for their willingness to cast aside personal goals and desires to carry out God's will during their lives on earth.

Conclusion

There are three different wills in this world - the will of God, the will of Satan and the will of man. We can rest assured the will of Satan and the will of man will be pulling at us at all times. We don't have to do anything for these two wills to be pulling at us. This comes naturally.

We must do a great deal to find, enter into and carry out God's will for our lives. Nothing is more important. We must not miss the reason for our lives. It's tragic to be sent to earth for a specific mission and to miss out on this completely.

It's not easy for us to see God's will clearly while we are on earth: "For now we are looking in a mirror that gives only a dim (blurred) reflection [of reality as in a riddle or enigma], but then [when perfection comes] we shall see in reality and face to face! Now I know in part (imperfectly); but then I shall know and understand fully and clearly, even in the same manner as I have been fully and clearly known and understood [by God]." (I Corinthians 13:12, *The Amplified Bible*)

Our vision here on earth is blurred by the pull of Satan and by the pull of the carnal nature we received from Adam. When we get to heaven, God's will for our lives will be clearly revealed. I hope this book will remove some of the blurriness and allow you to see God's will for your life much more clearly.

Jesus Christ paid a tremendous price for each of us. Every Christian will come face to face with Him in heaven. We don't want to come into His presence after a life full of wasted years doing what we wanted. Instead, we should want more than anything else to hear Him say "Well done, good and faithful servant."

We are His servants. He is the Master. We are not on earth to do our will. We are here to serve Him. We are here to carry out His will.

It's not too late to start living our lives the way He wants us to live them. Today is the first day of the rest of your life. This book is filled with specific instructions on how to find, enter into and remain in God's will.

It's not a book to be read. It is a book to be studied and thoroughly digested. I urge every reader to complete the quiz at the end of this book. See how much you have learned. Then go back and carefully study the areas you don't understand.

I pray that the specific instructions in this book will help you to find God's will for your life, enter into it and remain in it. Magnificent eternal rewards will await you if you are successful.

What Did You Learn From This Book?

One way of finding out how much you have retained from this book is to take the following test. How many answers do you know now - while this book is still fresh in your mind? I suggest that you mark your calendar to take this test again on a specific date - thirty to ninety days from now, to check your retention after a period of time.

This book will help you only to the degree that it can persuade you to change your habits to line up with the instructions that our Father has given us to follow if we want to learn how to find His will for our lives.

Question	Page Ref.
1. Does God have a definite plan for each of our lives before He creates us?	9
2. How intimately does our Creator know each person He has created?	10

13. What happened in the garden of Gethsemane that can teach us a great deal about the importance of carrying out God's will for our lives? 16-18

14. What price did Jesus pay for us when He was scourged by Roman soldiers? 18

15. What physical price did Jesus pay for us when He was crucified? 18

16. What price did Jesus pay through crucifixion that was even greater than His physical suffering? 19

17. Why do many Bible scholars believe God actually turned His back on Jesus when He was being crucified? 19

18. If we want to be true brothers and sisters of Jesus Christ, what should our primary goal be? 19

19. If we have been reborn spiritually, do we have a moral right to live our lives the way we want to live them? 20

20. What relationship do love and humility have to living our lives according to God's will? 21, 22

21. Why are we blind to God's will if we don't love others? 22

22. If we can't know God, we can't know His will. What one quality above all else is necessary to know God better? 22

23. How can Christians love people who are extremely difficult to love? 23

24. Why does pride block us from finding God's will? Why does humility open the door to God's will? 23, 24

25. Why do self-confidence and self-reliance make it very difficult to find God's will? 24, 25

26. When we rush ahead of God, what does this do to the power of the Holy Spirit? 25, 26

27. In the kingdom of God, what are leaders called to be? 27

28. Does it come naturally to us to seek God's will instead of our own goals? 27

29. As we grow older, why are we more likely to want to find God's will for our lives? 27, 28

30. If we truly belong to Jesus, what will we do with our personal goals? 28

31. What does it mean to be "crucified with Christ"? 29

32. If we want to escape the lure of sin, we must overcome the one quality that is at the root of all sin. What is this undesirable quality? 30

33. Why does Satan try to deceive us into believing God's will is unattractive? 31

34. Why shouldn't we be afraid of God's will? 32

35. Is God's will as beautiful in the valleys of life as it is on the mountaintops? 32

36. Is this world our real home? Where is our real home? 33

37. How can we experience a preview of the joy of heaven? 33, 34

38. Where does the Holy Spirit live? What does He want us to do with our God-given right to control our lives? 34

39. What will the Lord give us if we delight in Him and desire His will more than anything else? 34

40. How can we be assured that God will reveal His will to us? 35

41. Why is it so important for Christians to turn away from the ways of the world? If we like the world's way of doing things, what relationship does this put us into with God? 37, 38

42. Why is God so adamant about Christians' not conforming to the ways of the world? 38

43. If we live according to worldly customs, have we really died with Christ? 38

44. If we want to receive favor from God, what must we do regarding relationships with unbelievers? 39

45. Does this mean we shouldn't witness salvation to unbelievers? 39

46. What is the difference between the way the world sees things and the way God looks at us? 39, 40

47. Should we seek popularity with other people? Whom should we seek to please? 41

48. Is worldly wisdom of any advantage in finding God's will for our lives? 41

49. What does it mean to be "transformed" by the renewing of our minds? 43, 44

50. Why is it important to grow past spiritual infancy and to continue to mature if we want to find God's will? 44

51. How does renewing our minds help us to understand our rationalization? 44

52. What does God's Word say about the futility of human logic and reasoning in regard to His kingdom? 44

53. What does God's Word say about doing evil and our knowledge of Him? 44

54. Is there a relationship between spiritual maturity and the ability to stand firm in anything that is part of God's will? 45

55. How do we discard our former nature so that we are constantly renewed with a fresh mental and spiritual attitude? 45

56. Most of us cleanse our bodies with a daily bath or shower. How do we cleanse our souls? 45, 46

57. How can we restore what we lost through Adam, thus enabling us to find God's will? 46

58. How can we open a spiritual channel to God that will enable us to understand more concerning His will? 46, 47

59. As we approach middle age and old age, why is it even more important to renew our minds on a daily basis? 47

60. Before we can find God's specific will for our lives, what is necessary to find His general will? 49

61. When we come to a crossroads and don't know which way to go, what does God's Word tell us to do? 50

62. What do we need to do to escape the temptations of the world and to live the way God wants us to live? 50

63. What did God provide that is able to penetrate deep down inside of us to show us what we are really like? 50, 51

64. What does it mean to "abide" in God's Word? What benefits will we receive if we do this continuously? 51

65. What will happen to us when God's Word enters into our hearts? 51, 52

66. What does God want us to do if we can only see a short way ahead and we can't see very far into the future? 52

67. Many people exercise regularly to build up their bodies. What does God's Word tell us to do to build ourselves up spiritually? 52

68. What is necessary for us to get to the point where we are actually delighted to do God's will? 52

69. What does God's Word say about the penalty that faces people who ignore the instructions of His Word? 53

70. How can mere human beings understand the deep truths of God which are necessary to determine His will? 55

71. Instead of struggling and straining trying to carry out God's will with our human abilities, what should we do? 56

72. How can we escape the cravings and desires of the flesh? 56, 57

73. Where do we receive the power and the desire to carry out God's will? 57

74. How do we fall into a trap if we try to carry out God's will with our own abilities? 57

75. How can we tune in to the frequency that enables us to hear the still, small voice of the Holy Spirit? 58

76. How does the Holy Spirit actually speak to us and guide us? 58

77. Is it a good idea to start each morning with a prayer? What might this prayer include to receive guidance from the Holy Spirit during the upcoming day? 58, 59

89. Why can we expect persecution from worldly people if we do our very best to live according to God's will? 73, 74

90. How does God's Word tell us we should react when we are persecuted because we seek His will at all times? 74

91. When we are seeking God's will and we have to face a lot of adversity, why does He allow this to happen? 74, 75

92. Why do we have nothing to fear if we seek God's will with all our hearts? 75

93. What does it mean when someone says he will "set my face like flint to do His will?" 78

94. If we seek God's will, why is it so important for us to have strong and unwavering faith in Him? 79

95. Give three biblical examples of people who were in God's will and were brought safely through difficult problems? 80

96. When we seek God's will, why can we be completely confident in releasing our problems to Him knowing He will take care of them? 80

97. Jesus said He would carry our heavy loads for us if we would take His yoke upon us. What does this mean? 80, 81

98. When we pray to God for something that is not in His will, how does He look at these requests? 83

99. If we pray according to God's will, is there any question whatever that He hears our prayer? Does He hear our prayers when they are for our own sinful desires? 84

100. God's Word says that Jesus is our advocate and intercessor when we pray. What does this mean? 84, 85

101. If we know we have prayed according to God's will, and we know He heard our request, is there any doubt that He will answer if our faith is strong and enduring? 85

102. If we truly seek God's will, how often should we come to Him in prayer? 87

103. Many people miss God's will because they are busily chasing after pleasure. What does God's Word say about people who love pleasure? 89, 90

104. Can we find satisfaction through our five senses? 90

105. There is only one place where we can find complete satisfaction for our spiritual hunger and thirst. Where do we find this? 90

106. Do we dare throw our lives away for our Lord and turn away from goals that seem right to us? What does God's Word say will happen if we do this? 91

107. Instead of settling for the temporary pleasures of this world, where can we find fullness of joy and eternal pleasure? 91, 92

Appendix

Have You Entered Into The Kingdom Of God?

(Note: All Scripture references in this Appendix are from *The King James Bible* unless indicated otherwise.)

You have just read a complete summary of God's Word pertaining to the subject of His will for our lives. These are laws that our Father has written for His children - those human beings who have entered into His kingdom. I ask each reader of this book, "Have you entered into the kingdom of God?"

Jesus Christ said, "...Verily, verily, I say unto thee, Except a man be born again, he cannot see the kingdom of God." (John 3:3) Jesus went on to say, "...Ye must be born again." (John 3:7) It is very clear that there is only one way to enter into the kingdom of God and that is to be "born again."

We don't enter into God's kingdom by church attendance, by teaching Sunday School, by baptism, by confirmation or by living a good life. Jesus Christ paid the price for every one of us to enter into God's kingdom, but this is not "automatic." Many people are so caught up with their own religious denomination or their own personal beliefs that they completely miss God's specific instructions as to how to enter into His kingdom - for the rest of our lives on earth and also for eternity in heaven.

To become a born-again Christian, we first of all, must admit that we are sinners (Romans 3:23, James 2:10). We must admit that there is absolutely no way that we can enter into God's kingdom based upon our own merits. Next, we have to genuinely repent of our sins (Luke 13:3, Acts 3:19).

After this admission of sin and repentance, there is one additional step that we must take to become a born-again Christian: "For if you tell others with your own mouth that Jesus Christ is your Lord, and believe in your own heart that God has raised Him from the dead, you will be saved. For it is by believing in his heart that a man becomes right with God; and with his mouth he tells others of his faith, confirming his salvation." (Romans 10:9-10, *The Living Bible*)

Many people know that Jesus Christ died for our sins. However, knowledge isn't enough. Intellectual agreement isn't enough. To be born again, we have to accept Jesus as our Saviour in our hearts and not just in our heads. We're not born again until we come to Him as admitted sinners and trust Him deep down in our hearts as the only way that we can enter into the kingdom of God. God knows exactly what we believe deep down in our hearts (I Sammuel 16:7, I Chronicles 28:9, Hebrews 4:13).

We must believe in our hearts that Jesus Christ is the Son of God, that He was born of a virgin, that He died on the cross to pay for our sins, that He rose again from the dead and that He lives today. To be a born-again Christian, Romans 10:9-10 tells us that we must not only believe this in our hearts, but we also must open our mouths and tell others of this belief. This confirms our salvation.

When you believe this in your heart and tell others of this belief with your mouth, then you are a born-again Christian. All of us were born naturally on the day that our mothers gave birth to us. We must have a second birth - a spiritual birth - to enter into God's kingdom: "For you have a new life. It was not passed on to you from your parents, for the life they gave you will fade away. This new one will last forever, for it comes from Christ, God's ever-living Message to men." (I Peter 1:23, *The Living Bible*)

God wants us to come to Him, not as intellectuals, but as little children. God doesn't reveal Himself to us through our intellects. He reveals Himself to us through our hearts and to enter into His kingdom, we must come to Him as little children. We may be adults in the natural world, but in the spiritul world we have to start all over. We have to be born again as spiritual babies. Jesus said, "...Except ye be converted, and become as little children, ye shall not enter into the kingdom of heaven." (Matthew 18:3)

The following prayer will cause you to become born again if you believe this in your heart and open your mouth and tell others of this belief:

> "Dear Father, I come to You in the Name of Jesus Christ. I admit that I am a sinner and I know there is no way that I can enter into Your kingdom based upon the sinful life that I have led. I'm genuinely sorry for my sins and I ask for Your mercy. I believe in my heart that Jesus Christ is Your Son - that He was born of a virgin, that He died on the cross to pay for my sins, that You raised Him from the dead and that He is alive today. I trust in Him as my only way of entering into Your kingdom. I confess now to You, Father, that Jesus Christ is my Saviour and my Lord and I will tell others of this decision now and in the future. Thank You, Father. Amen."

When you believe this in your heart and confess this to others with your mouth, you have been reborn spiritually. You are brand new in the spiritual realm: "Therefore if any man be in Christ, he is a new creature: old things are passed away; behold, all things are become new." (II Corinthians 5:17)

Now that you have a new recreated spirit, you are ready to study, understand and obey God's laws pertaining to His will for your life and all of His other laws. This will transform the rest of your life on earth and you will also live forever in heaven: "For God so loved the world, that he gave his only Son, that whosoever believeth in him should not perish, but have everlasting life." (John 3:16)

Other Books by Jack Hartman

CONQUERING FEAR

The last days before Jesus Christ returns are very close. Difficult times are ahead of us. Fear will increase significantly during that time. Many Christians who are now secure through various forms of worldly security will lose what has sheltered them from fear. They will almost be consumed by fear.

Jack Hartman knows what it is to be paralyzed by fear. He has had to deal with a great deal of fear in his life. Because of this, he has spent thousands of hours studying the Bible to learn what It teaches about overcoming fear. This book does not contain his personal opinions. Each principle for overcoming fear is based solidly upon the Word of God.

If you are unable to find these titles at your local Christian bookstore there is an order form provided at the end of the book.

Jack Hartman is a self-employed businessman. In 1974, he was on the verge of bankruptcy and a nervous breakdown. He was almost paralyzed by worry and fear. At that time he accepted Jesus Christ as Saviour and Lord.

He immediately started to study and meditate day and night in the Holy Scriptures to learn how to solve his financial and emotional problems. After several months of study he was able to apply these Biblical principles to his problems and they worked!

His business has turned completely around, all debts have been paid off right on schedule and his business has grown steadily each year since then. In addition, he and three other businessmen started a Bible study class in his office which now has grown into a large church with average Sunday morning attendance of 1,000 people.

The growth of this business and the growth of this church have come as a result of applying Biblical principles which Jack has explained in his book *Trust God For Your Finances.*

The principles in this book are not theoretical. They have worked in Jack Hartman's life and in the lives of many people who have counseled with him. Now these principles are available in book form.

Jack carefully points out the differences between the world's system of prosperity and God's laws of prosperity. He explains that all of the warnings in the Bible against financial prosperity are warnings against following the *world's* system of prosperity.

Our Father very *definitely* wants His children to prosper as long as they follow His laws of prosperity. These laws are laid out in detail in sixteen chapters of specific instruction - every chapter filled with many verses of Scripture.

As soon as Jack accepted Christ as his personal Saviour, he began an intensive study of God's Word. From the very first day of this study and meditation the Lord led him to write "Spiritual Meditations" on the Spiritual truths that he learned that day. He now has written over 40,000 (!) of these meditations and he continues to write them almost every day of his life.

Jack has now written a book of his best Spiritual meditations on the subject of faith. The title of this book is *Nuggets Of Faith*. There are over eighty of these "nuggets" (average length - 3 paragraphs) which are the result of thousands of hours of research and study.

There are no wasted words in this book. Each of these "nuggets" goes straight to the point. This book will give you maximum results in a minimum of time. It will make you think.

You can easily read this book in one day. On the other hand, each of these "nuggets" contains enough depth so that you can take one "nugget" with you in the morning and dwell on it throughout the day, turning its Scriptural truth over and over in your mind as you meditate on how this Scriptural truth can apply to your life.

As a Bible study teacher and a Christian counselor, Jack has encountered many worried, anxious and fearful people over the years. They worry about family problems... health problems... employment problems... The list goes on and on.

However, our Lord Jesus told us not to be worried, troubled or afraid. He wouldn't have told us this if it were impossible to do.

Despite the adversity He faced, Jesus didn't worry. Although He has given this same peace to us to sustain us during our trials and tribulations, receiving this peace is not "automatic". It is actually similar to money in a bank account. Jesus made the "deposit" of peace for us, but we have to learn to make "withdrawals".

Deep Inner Peace is an in-depth study of what the Bible has to say about God-given peace. The principles in this book are not theoretical. They have worked successfully in Jack Hartman's life and the lives of many people who have followed these principles.

Jack carefully points out the differences between the world's ideas of peace and the *deep inner peace* that comes from knowing Christ, the Prince of peace. He believes that God's Word clearly sets forth the formula for true, lasting peace. These principles are laid out in detail in eighteen chapters of Scriptural truth. The book closes with a unique "test" in which readers may test themselves on their knowledge of God's *deep inner peace*. It is the author's sincere belief that you can never be the same after reading this book and giving yourself this test.

One thing that is obvious about Jack Hartman is his deep love for the Word of God. Ever since his close brush with personal bankruptcy and a nervous breakdown, he has devoted his life to the study of the Scriptures. Nothing is more exciting to Jack than to receive fresh, new truths from God's Word.

How To Study The Bible explains the specific method that Jack uses to study God's Word. It has worked successfully for him and the students in his Bible study classes. Many letters have been received from all over the world commenting on the effectiveness of this method of Bible study.

The importance of studying God's Word is made clear in the Scriptures. Not only does Jack show why God says we must study His Word - he also gives definite, step-by-step instructions for the method he uses.

Jack has found that many people try to study God's Word, only to give up after awhile, confused and frustrated. *How To Study The Bible* carefully explains a proven, effective method that will help any reader to learn how to solve specific problems in his or her life.

Jack's system of Bible study is easy to understand, but involves a lot of hard work and discipline. However, the rewards of studying God's Word make it well worth the effort.

In his early years as a Bible study teacher, Jack Hartman saw the necessity of an easy-to-read book that unsaved people could read, showing them their need for salvation. As a result, *One Hundred Years From Today* was written in Bible study form and was made available to those who attended Jack's Bible study classes. Now it has been revised and printed as a book and is available to all of Jack's readers.

One Hundred Years From Today is the perfect witnessing tool. After pointing out that every word in the Bible is inspired by God Himself, Jack goes on to explain what salvation is... why we must be saved... how to become saved... where we will be one hundred years from today if we are saved - and if we are not.

This book uses simple language to clearly show that there are two roads that can be taken and that we must make our decision while we're alive on this earth. Jack warns the reader not to trust in religion or in good works in order to get to heaven. He makes it very clear that *Jesus is the only way.*

The reason for the effectiveness of this Scripture-packed study is Jack's conversational style. He spares the complex theological language, gets right to the point and makes an appeal to the reader to pray a sinner's prayer. You can be assured that, upon finishing this book, the reader will have been told the message of salvation through Jesus Christ.

Hundreds of people have come to know Jesus as a result of reading *One Hundred Years From Today* when it was in Bible study form, and many more will receive Jesus as Lord and Saviour now that it has been published.

Soaring Above The Problems Of Life is a Scripture-packed study that explains why we as Christians go through trials and tribulations, how to respond to them and how they can actually *benefit* us.

The Word of God doesn't always tell us *why* things happen the way they do. However, it does tell us how to respond to these situations. It teaches us how to respond God's way, instead of reacting to problems the way that the world does. If we learn to respond the way our Father wants us to, our problems will affect us less and less.

This book will help you if you are going through a difficult time. Even if you are *not* having any trials right now, this book is still a necessity because Jesus said that all of us will go through trials and tribulations. We should use our "summertime" - the time when things are going well in our lives - to gather an abundant harvest of Spiritual truth to store up in our hearts for the "winter" days that are sure to come.

Soaring Above The Problems Of Life is not just a book to be read. It is meant to be studied... marked up... highlighted and underlined. In fact, you will find a quiz at the end of the book so that you can test yourself to find out how much of it you have retained.

ORDER FORM

Books	Qty.	Price
Trust God For Your Finances ($4.95)	____	$ ______
Nuggests Of Faith ($2.50)	____	$ ______
Deep Inner Peace ($4.95)	____	$ ______
How To Study The Bible ($3.50)	____	$ ______
100 Years From Today ($2.95)	____	$ ______
Soaring Above The Problems Of Life ($5.95)	____	$ ______
Conquering Fear ($5.95)	____	$ ______

Enclosed Check or Money Order $ ______
(Please do not send cash)

Make check payable to: New Leaf Press
Mail order to: P.O. Box 311
Green Forest, AR 72638

Please print your name and address **clearly:**

Name ____

Address ____

City ____

State or Province ____

Zip or Postal Code ____

Foreign orders must be submitted in U.S. dollars.
Foreign orders are shipped by uninsured surface mail. We ship all orders within 48 hours of receipt of order.

M/C-Visa — Call toll free 1-800-643-9535